JACOB ARMINIUS

CASCADE COMPANIONS

The Christian theological tradition provides an embarrassment of riches: from scripture to modern scholarship, we are blessed with a vast and complex theological inheritance. And yet this feast of traditional riches is too frequently inaccessible to the general reader.

The Cascade Companions series addresses the challenge by publishing books that combine academic rigor with broad appeal and readability. They aim to introduce nonspecialist readers to that vital storehouse of authors, documents, themes, histories, arguments, and movements that comprise this heritage with brief yet compelling volumes.

JACOB ARMINIUS

The Man from Oudewater

RUSTIN E. BRIAN

CASCADE *Books* • Eugene, Oregon

JACOB ARMINIUS
The Man from Oudewater

Cascade Companions

Cascade Books
An Imprint of Wipf and Stock Publishers
199 W. 8th Ave., Suite 3
Eugene, OR 97401

www.wipfandstock.com

ISBN 13: 978-1-4982-1976-1

Cataloguing-in-Publication Data

Brian, Rustin Emery.

Jacob Arminius : the man from Oudewater / Rustin E. Brian

xii + 114 p. ; 23 cm. Includes bibliographical references.

ISBN 13: 978-1-4982-1976-1

Cascade Companions 17

1. Arminius, Jacobus, 1560–1609. 2. Arminianism. 3. I. Title. 2. Series.

BX6195 .B74 2015

09/03/2015

To Rev. Thomas Vance Findlay
Thank you for sharing your books and, more
importantly, your life.

CONTENTS

ACKNOWLEDGMENTS

THE COMPLETION OF THIS book was dependent upon many good friends whom I would be remiss not to thank. First thanks go to Tom Findlay who upon learning that I wanted to study Arminius's theology, amassed a veritable library of rare, old, and quite valuable books to help in my work. Tom did not live to see this book's completion, but he is alive on every page. Special thanks also go to Point Loma Nazarene University and to Mark Mann for both allowing me to present (and more importantly to learn) at the Rethinking Arminius Conference in 2012, and for hosting my family during the summer of 2014 at the Wesleyan Center on campus. Over half of this book was written at PLNU. Thanks also to Lydia Heberling, and to the rest of the summer scholars and PLNU faculty and staff that assisted me and discussed Arminius with me—thanks! This book was also written at several other locations, including the home of my parents, Randy and Barbara Brian, my in-laws, Bryan and Laura Ellis, the church where I am fortunate enough to serve as pastor, Renton Church of the Nazarene, and the library at Seattle Pacific University. Thank you also to Preston Goff, Mark Mann, and Cody Stauffer who were kind enough to read portions of the working manuscript and offer advice. Thank you to my family, to my beautiful, kind, strong, and patient wife, Lauren; my fiery, passionate, and bold little girl, Lily; and my big, happy, and growing boy, Rowan. Thanks for dealing with conferences, deadlines, and the almost constant need to go and write. You are a blessing to me in ways I can never describe. Thank you. Finally, thank you to my publisher, Cascade Books, for taking yet another chance on this young scholar. Specifically, thanks to Christian Amondson for your help and for believing in this project.

PREFACE

In 1575 most of the inhabitants of Oudewater, Holland, were brutally killed when Spanish Catholics assaulted the small Dutch town, which had recently converted to Protestantism. Arminius's mother and many siblings were killed in the massacre. Arminius, who was fifteen at the time, escaped death because he was away studying at Marburg. We know that Arminius made a visit to the decimated town *en route* from Marburg to Rotterdam, and that he maintained connections with a few who remained and resettled in Oudewater, including an aunt. Despite not returning to live in Oudewater, I would contend that narrowly escaping the gruesome fate of so many of his family and friends left a lasting effect upon Arminius.

With this as a backdrop, I propose to outline the life and theology of Jacob Arminius, shedding fresh light on the Dutch reformer's life and theology, in hopes that contemporary readers might discern just what it means to stand in the "Arminian" tradition today. In short, my hope is that readers of this introductory text will discover or rediscover the man behind the adjective.

Finally, as I read Arminius, his is a theology that is thoroughly unconcerned with being either "Reformed" or "Catholic." The resulting catholic, or broadly-Christian, theology is one that is shaped and guided first and foremost by Scripture, as well as deeply pastoral concerns. In this way, Arminius, and the resulting "tradition" that he births, stands as a *via media* tradition between the two dominant pillars of Roman Catholic and Reformed theology. Arminius's theology, thus, shares many points of agreement with Reformed theology, Lutheran theology, and Roman Catholic theology, but in a decidedly unintentional manner. My hope is to weave this together in a way that logically stems from his early experiences of loss as connected to the two dominant theological positions of his day: Reformed and Roman Catholic theology.

PART 1

WHO WAS ARMINIUS?

Chapter 1

INTRODUCTION

The Man behind the Adjective

THIS BOOK IS WRITTEN from a Wesleyan and catholic, and therefore an Arminian, perspective. I was not always a Wesleyan, though. Like many North Americans from the United States, my young faith was a strange amalgamation of fundamentalism and civil religion. When pushed, my theology typically drew upon what I now know to be Calvinistic categories of the Baptist persuasion, as well as woefully inadequate eschatology—or the doctrine of last things. It was not until my late teenage years that I encountered Wesleyan theology. I quickly and fully embraced it. It was then that I began to hear talk of "Wesleyan-Arminian" theology. But who was this Arminius character? The best answer I could give at the time was that he believed in free will. In a very real way, then, Arminius was, for me, simply the mysterious source of a modifying adjective.

Perhaps I was just a poor student, but my ignorance of Arminius held sway all the way through doctoral studies. In fact, it was only during a year spent at the University of Aberdeen, a Scottish Institution with highly Reformed sensibilities, that I encountered regular discussions regarding Arminius. In that setting, Arminius (and therefore Wesley)

3

was commonly viewed as being either semi- or fully-Pelagian. My attempts to counter such critiques led me to realize that I knew nothing, really, about Arminius: both the man and his theology. It is my belief that, though the specifics of my experiences are unique, the overall condition of knowledge—or more accurately, lack of knowledge—about Arminius, is all too common in so-called Wesleyan-Arminian circles. This is unfortuante, for Arminius provides a rich and powerful theological backdrop that renders Wesley's pastoral and homiletical theology all the more profound. In a very real way, Arminius provides the rigorous systematic theology necessary for Wesley's theology. Thus, while it is appropriate to use Arminius's name adjectivally to modify Wesleyan theology, it is more appropriate to say that Wesley's theology depends upon Arminius's theology, and is to its very core thoroughly Arminian.

It is appropriate that in the eighteenth century Wesley sought for religious renewal within the Anglican Church, and ended up changing the entire world, for Arminius did something quite similar in the sixteenth century. Arminius lived at a turbulent time of world-changing and destructive religious tension. He grew up and was trained in the midst of constant theological battles between Reformation Protestants and Counter-Reformation Roman Catholics. Additionally, he saw firsthand the all-too-real effects of the theopolitical colonizing efforts of the Spanish Inquisition. His hometown of Oudewater, for example, was completely destroyed. Those who did not flee were brutally massacred by Spanish Catholics in 1575. Amidst such a brutal reality, Arminius refused to toe the major party lines. Rather, he dove deeply into Scripture, and stood firmly on what he found there. In particular, Arminius was convinced that much of the theology of the day made God out to be the author of evil, something Arminius worked tirelessly to

4

reject. Engaging the work of Arminius, therefore, can be a dangerous thing. He challenged the categories of thought held so firmly by many of Christ's followers in ways that always seemed to invite controversy. Arminius himself was constantly scrutinized for his theological beliefs and teachings. This was particularly true of his time as a professor. Though his theology spread like wild fire, Arminians faced that same scrutiny as well, for both Calvinistic Reformed theology and Roman Catholic theology continued to, for the most part, serve as the theology of choice for those in power in Europe.[1] Despite having the momentum of several centuries of the flourishing of Arminian theology, John Wesley faced similar criticism and scrutiny in his revival movement in Britain. Even the early Puritan settlers of the so-called "new world" that would eventually become the United States of America outlawed Arminian theology.[2]

Rediscovering, or discovering Arminius's theology, is a worthwhile pursuit. It is to this end that the first section of the book will be committed. My primary goal is quite simple: to provide an accessible introduction to Jacob Arminius's life and theology. My attention to brevity and accessibility will surely leave some wanting more. Fortunately, there are several wonderful works that provide much more detail on these subjects that readers can engage for further

1. González points out that Arminianism became, basically, the theology of the masses, whereas Calvinism was commonly the theology of the elite. *A History of Christian Thought*, 283.

2. This, of course, demonstrates that the earliest intention behind freedom of religion in the United States was not freedom *for*, but rather freedom *from*—Arminianism (which included Anglicanism) and Roman Catholicism. Thus, any effort to maintain that the foundation of the United States is a "Christian nation" must, in the least, admit that it was, at best, a vision of a very particular form of Calvinistic Christianity that these early settlers had in mind. Bangs, *Arminius: A Study in the Dutch Reformation*, 159.

study. The most thorough and helpful biography of Jacob Arminius is Carl Bangs's classic, *Arminius: A Study in the Dutch Reformation*. Bangs's book is the gold standard for biographical work on Arminius and is surely the next stop for anyone desiring further knowledge about the life of Arminius. A much more recent book, *Jacob Arminius: Theologian of Grace*, written by Keith D. Stanglin and Thomas H. McCall, provides a wonderfully detailed and well-written summary of Arminius's basic theological positions. Reading the collected works of Jacob Arminius is the best place to learn Arminius's theology, but Stanglin and McCall provide a very thorough and robust summary of Arminius's major theological points.

A second motivating factor behind writing this book is pastoral. My hope is that this book will help to provide pastors, students, and interested lay people with a cursory understanding of Arminius's life and theology, and thus with a different theological framework from which to engage both Scripture and the world. Arminius's theology is a theology of grace and hope, grounded solely in the life, death, resurrection, and ascension of Jesus Christ. As such, Arminius's theology is thoroughly Trinitarian and consistently christological. Arminius's sustained Christology is refreshing and helpful in formulating how a Christian might engage sin, suffering, and death.

Too often those from allegedly Wesleyan and Arminian backgrounds resort to heavily Reformed categories in explaining and engaging issues of theodicy (Why do evil or bad things happen?). For example, the death of a loved one often prompts such language as, "The good Lord knew it was Grandma's time," or, "I'm not sure why, but God decided it was time to take my little boy." The same line of reasoning can be seen when a TV preacher declares that a natural disaster killing thousands was God's will against "those people." Surely God did not decide to kill a young boy, "take" Grandma, or wipe out thousands of people through a fire, earthquake, typhoon, or especially a terrorist attack! This is a highly Reformed way of looking at theodicy and, as Arminius would argue, renders God the author of evil.[3] Instead, Arminius helps us to see that God is not the formal cause of such things. God does indeed allow such things to happen (Arminius might say that God has "middle knowledge" of such events), but this is because God has created a world, and humans in particular, with true freedom. Doing away with the negative results of our freedom—sin and death—would negate freedom in the first place, something Arminius was determined not to do. Attributing (malicious) causality to God for loss, suffering, and tragedy seems to be comforting to many people. This is not, however, consistent with Arminius's theology, nor, I would argue, the Bible. Arminius provides a better pastoral way to understand difficult situations without making God the cause of such evil and thus a more helpful way to care for others through tragedy and loss.

Finally, after examining the life and theology of Jacob Arminius, I will turn to a discussion of Arminian theology today. This concluding section will in no way exhaust

3. It is important to not equate Calvin here with "Reformed" theology (at least on this matter), for Calvin did not necessarily teach all the things that the later Calvinists taught. A common and helpful distinction can be drawn between Calvin and the Synod of Dort. Post-Dortian Calvinists taught things such as supralapsarian double-predestination in Calvin's name (in short, that, prior to creation, God willed that some would be saved and others damned, regardless of their actions and beliefs), something that Calvin avoided. We will examine this with greater detail in section II, chapter 7 in particular, but suffice it to say that in this work I will intentionally draw a distinction between Calvin himself and Reformed theology. The latter I take to include, and perhaps draw more heavily upon, the Synod of Dort than even Calvin himself.

the topic. Instead, my hope is to look at Arminius's theology in conjunction with a few major theological figures in particular: Pelagius, Wesley, and Barth. My hope is to further clarify Arminian theology by looking at Arminius's theology in conjunction with and in contrast to a few major thinkers. The book will then conclude with a chapter on "what it means to be Arminian today," in which I will argue for a renewed and intentional embrace of the theology of Jacob Arminius: in the pulpit, the pew, and the classroom.

Arminius's theology holds together God's utter sovereignty and the freedom of humanity both to be open toward God and to turn away from God. It also maintains that, through grace, humans can turn toward God as well, freely receiving God's favor and blessing. And while this is a grace-dependent move, the grace necessary for such a turn is not arbitrary or limited. Instead, Arminius, and those who claim his theology as their own, affirms that, despite the total depravity of humanity, God's grace is always already present in and to creation, allowing for humans in particular to turn toward God. This is a theological sensibility worth holding on to—worth rediscovering. I suspect, though, that even this brief description may come as somewhat of a surprise to many who might consider themselves Wesleyan and Arminian (Wesley, too, affirmed total depravity).

We must recover the theology of Jacob Arminius. We must move beyond the mere use of an adjective, to the intentional use of the name of Arminius to identify with a rich and robust theological framework. Similarly, Bangs argues that Arminius now functions as a "digit"—"something which must be placed in the equation, but not the object of separate attention."[4] In the end, whether readers embrace or reject the theology of Jacob Arminius, such a pursuit will

4. Bangs, *Arminius: A Study in the Dutch Reformation*, 19.

clearly lay out differences and, perhaps, unforeseen similarities between different theological traditions. Arminius was a faithful Christian who was profoundly catholic in his teaching. He was a faithful follower of Christ who sought to understand his pursuit of Jesus through a rigorous devotion to Scripture. More than anything else, Scripture guided his faith and, therefore, his theology. Arminius was not concerned with being Reformed or Roman Catholic, but with being faithfully Christian. An embrace of Arminius's theology is, therefore, an embrace of the impulse of fidelity to Scripture alone as it reveals to us the person and work of Jesus Christ. This is no bibliolatry, but rather the embrace of a particular theological exegesis of Scripture, where the complexity of the entire biblical witness is allowed precedence over any system or agenda. Arminius's theology is biblical theology. It is careful, logical, and systematic, but it is biblical throughout. It is consistent with classical interpretation of Scripture and it is, therefore, relevant today. Before we arrive at that conclusion, however, we must begin with a look at the early life of Jacob Arminius, the man from Oudewater.

FOR DISCUSSION

1. Why might it be important for Wesleyans in particular to discover (or re-discover) Arminius?

2. Why was it important to Arminius that God not be the author of evil? How does Rustin Brian suggest that evil is related to human freedom?

3. Why is it suggested that Arminius come to serve as more than simply an adjective?

Chapter 2

ARMINIUS'S EARLY LIFE

Jacob Harmenszoon was born in 1559 in Oudewater, Holland. Following the custom of his day, Jacob later Latinized his name, adopting the name Jacobus Arminius. His father Harmen Jacobsz died the same year, leaving his wife to raise their three or four children.[1] Arminius's mother appears to have been named Elborch, a name that quickly fell out of use with the rise of Protestantism in Holland. In its place, the name Elgetje, or Angelica in English, was used. Some changed their names, while others had their name changed, unwillingly, in the annals of history by Protestant historians. Such is likely the case with Arminius's mother. Even more uncertainty surrounds Elborch's past, as almost

---

1. The precise number of Arminius's siblings is somewhat unclear. Bangs notes that records show Jacob likely had two siblings, one brother and one sister. This is supported by Bertius's funeral oration (Bangs, *Arminius*, 29). Contrarily, Bangs quotes Casper Brandt, author of the primary English biography of Arminius that circulated for roughly 200 years, who states in his *Historie der Reformatie* that Jacob had a sister and two brothers. Curiously, though, in Brandt's aforementioned *Life of Arminius*, Brandt states about Jacob, "He lost his father in infancy; and his mother, thus prematurely deprived of her partner, was left, with the three children she had by him, to pass her widowed days in somewhat straitened circumstances." Brandt, *The Life of James Arminius*, 13.

nothing is known about her today, save that she was mother to Jacob and wife to Harmen. We do know that Harmen was a weapons maker, or armorer, an occupation that granted him some significance in the small but important town of Oudewater. Beyond this, not much is known of Arminius's family history. Carl Bangs points out the possibility that Arminius's great uncle was Heer Jan Claesz van Leiden, who was a nobleman and, most likely, a Catholic priest. Indeed, it is difficult to make definitive claims about Arminius's ancestry, except to say that he did come from a family of some significance. "It seems quite possible that Arminius did not come from an obscure family, and that may be one reason that he came to the attention of a series of benefactors who made sure that he had access to the best education available."[2]

Following the death of Arminius's father, Harmen, a local priest named Theodore Aemilius offered his financial support and assumed responsibility for the young Arminius's education. Aemilius had Protestant sympathies, though it was unclear if he was openly a Protestant or not, as Oudewater did not officially become a Protestant town until 1574. At some point, Arminius likely went to live with Aemilius in Utrecht, a town roughly twenty-nine kilometers northeast of Oudewater. There, it is believed that he attended the St. Jerome School. Aemilius's impact upon young Arminius cannot be overstated. Aemilius's support and care, in lieu of Arminius's father, was surely a help to the young boy. Aemilius opened academic doors to Arminius as well, doors that may not have otherwise opened to him. In many ways Aemilius both gave young Arminius a future and, quite literally, saved his life. Aemilius died sometime in late 1574 or early 1575, leaving Arminius in need once more. Eventually, help came in the form of Rudolphus Snellius,

2. Bangs, *Arminius*, 29.

a scholar from the University of Marburg. Snellius became acquainted with Arminius during a visit to Utrecht, inviting Arminius back to Marburg with him, and offering a place at the university. Arminius made the journey to Marburg in the summer of 1575, and thus barely escaped the horrific events that befell the city of his birth just a few months later.

Holland quickly became polarized between Roman Catholicism and Reformed Protestantism. The former was championed by the Spanish regent, the Duke of Alva, and had all the trappings of colonialism. The latter found its hero in William of Orange. Coupled with the push for Reformed Protestantism was the desire for nationalism. Taking advantage of a decrease in Spanish troops that had been enforcing and charged with maintaining Roman Catholicism, a small force of Reformed mercenaries and noblemen entered Oudewater in June 1573 and enacted a small revolution. For a little over a year Reformed Protestants ruled the city. Catholics certainly remained, but they no longer had any control over government and worship. The hold of the Roman Catholic Church, as well as the Spanish efforts at colonization, rapidly came toward an end. Unwilling to give up, the Spanish engaged in one last push to muster renewed political and religious control over Holland. This series of battles was complicated by the fact that a large percentage of the Spanish forces were mercenaries. As Spain's control waned, these mercenaries were increasingly prone to pursue their own causes and to preserve their own interests. Brutality increased as Spanish control decreased. The ensuing battle is billed as a "religious" one, but this is not entirely accurate, as it was equally a political battle for nationalism and independence from tyrannical colonial rule. Assigning motivation for the battle is further complicated by the fact that so many of the combatants on the Spanish side were mercenaries looking out for their own interest, and in search of blood, sexual domination, and, in general, the spoils of war. It is important to remember that at that time it was very difficult to separate politics from religion, especially as Christianity was incarnated within the various systems of colonialism. Within such a system, Christianity often became a tool to be used by political leaders to accomplish their own agenda—whether peaceful or destructive. Such was the sort of religion that Marx would famously call the "opiate of the masses."

Little is known of the details of the Battle of Oudewater, save that it was brief and that the Spanish efforts at carnage and destruction were incredibly thorough. After having the conditions of surrender rejected by the town's government, the siege began on August 7, 1575. Bangs briefly and powerfully recounts the little that is known about the battle.

> It is not a nice story. First the defending soldiers on the walls were shot or stabbed to death. Those who fled into the town were pursued and killed. Then the massacre spread to noncombatants. Mothers were killed in front of their children; children in front of their mothers. Girls and women were raped in view of fathers and husbands, and then all were killed. No place, no person, was exempt from the pillaging invaders. When nuns in the cloisters were discovered, they pleaded that they were faithful Roman Catholics. "So much the better for your souls," said the soldiers as they raped and murdered them.[3]

Of the few accounts that remain of the battle, it is very difficult to say whether they are accurate, or whether they are embellished. All accounts, though, detail the sheer senseless brutality of the "battle," which really was a massacre. A

3. Ibid., 42.

few of the town's citizens obviously escaped death, but only by fleeing from the city. Arminius's aunt was one such survivor. Unfortunately, the same cannot be said for the rest of Arminius's family. Arminius's mother and his siblings were all killed in the battle of Oudewater. Having already lost his father, the rest of Arminius's family was brutally taken from him in one day, the result of senseless theopolitical violence. Bertius tells us in his funeral oration to Arminius that young Jacob spent two weeks in Marburg in constant tears before finally deciding to return to Oudewater to look upon the devastation with his own eyes. Though it was now a wasteland, Oudewater would have been under Spanish control when Arminius returned home. It was, therefore, a very risky trip. When he left Oudewater Arminius returned to Marburg, but only briefly. Soon, he would depart Marburg for the University at Leiden.

The effects of such a disturbing and painful loss upon Arminius are unknown. Surprisingly, he does not process through the events and their effect upon him in his journal. It would be impossible to think, though, that the loss of Arminius's family in such an unexpected and brutal way would not have an effect upon Arminius. During his two weeks of tears, as well as the countless times that the fate of his family must have haunted him in later years, I'm confident that Arminius was reminded of the reason for their murder. Many people in Oudewater had undergone a change in their theological persuasion, and were thus joining the new Reformed Church and leaving behind Roman Catholicism. A mere shift in their belief system suddenly made the city's inhabitants candidates for mass rape and murder—all, somehow, in the name of Jesus Christ. That is the most difficult part of trying to understand such events that are, unfortunately, all too common throughout history: those on both "sides" agreed on so very much, including the centrality of Jesus Christ. In fact, they agreed on far, far more than they disagreed upon. And yet, the disagreement was enough to cause widespread carnage.

I will come back to this, but it is important, at this point, to consider the direction that Arminius's theology went in light of this horrific event in his early life. Arminius was decidedly not a Roman Catholic. His critiques of the Roman Church were clear and strong. And yet, he was often criticized for secretly being a Catholic. This criticism came, in large part, because of his strong views on grace and human freedom. On the other hand, though, Arminius was rigidly opposed to some of the central tenets of Protestant Reformed theology. For Arminius, such theology was often devoid of grace, and, most importantly, God ended up being a cruel tyrant. In short, Arminius was not happy with either option. He certainly was not interested in toeing the party lines of either. Instead, using Scripture rather than reactionary doctrine or polity as his guide, Arminius walked a middle path—a *via media*. This was a truly difficult path to walk, for it risked the attacks of both of the major Christian sensibilities of his day.[4]

It makes sense to think that after the battle of Oudewater, Arminius would never be interested in strongly defending one ecclesiastical system over the other. His birthplace was destroyed by Catholics, while the birthplaces of others were destroyed by Protestants. Lives were fractured and destroyed by the very thing that was supposed to help provide stability, peace, and purpose. Arminius knew this pain firsthand and for that reason walked a different path, skirting the pitfalls of both Reformed and Catholic theology. Arminius was from Oudewater, a town whose

---

4. This is not to discount Eastern Orthodoxy, but simply to point out that Arminius lived in the "West," and therefore would have had very little contact with Eastern Orthodoxy.

inhabitants, including Arminius's mother and siblings, were beaten, raped, and brutally murdered for a change in their theological sensibilities. He would always be a man from Oudewater. He would always carry this tragic reality with him. How could he not?

Leaving the rubble of Oudewater behind him, Arminius traveled back to Marburg, where he would study for another year, before enrolling at the newly established University at Leiden in 1576. At Leiden, Arminius studied the Liberal Arts: mathematics, logic, theology, and Hebrew in particular. It was in Leiden, upon the occasion of his enrollment, that he first used the name "Jacobus Arminius."[5] Arminius's time at Leiden was marked by controversy and strong tension between Protestant and Roman Catholic professors. This controversy was mirrored by the churches in Leiden. At the center of the controversy both in the University and the city was pastor and theologian Caspar Coolhaes, who was raised and educated as a Roman Catholic, but who converted to Protestantism at the age of twenty-four. Coolhaes's conversion was heavily influenced by humanism, and as such his Protestantism was very moderate and appealing to a wide swath of people. He represented a theological middle ground of sorts, a way of thinking that proved a significant influence on the young Arminius. Eventually, in 1582, Coolhaes was deposed from ministry by the Provincial Synod of Haarlem, who deemed him to be not Protestant nor Reformed enough. The burgomasters, or town leaders of Leiden, though, refused to cease their support of Coolhaes. They continued to pay him, until Coolhaes established an alternate means of providing for his family: running a distillery. He remained heavily involved in the church and even wrote on theology and distilling.[6]

5. Cited in ibid., 47.
6. Ibid., 54–55.

Upon completing his studies in Leiden, Arminius gained the financial support of the Burgomasters of Amsterdam for further theological training. In exchange, they required his commitment to serve the church in Amsterdam upon the completion of his academic studies. Their financial support allowed him to go to Geneva, where he matriculated in January of 1582. At Geneva, Arminius came in contact with Calvin's theological heir, Theodore Beza. Beza took Calvin's theology to a new and even more rigid level. In particular, he made predestination a theological focus, stating that it preceded the decree of creation. Thus, for Beza the punishment for sin can be said to precede sin itself. Beza's intensification of Calvin's theology would reach its culmination at the Synod of Dort in 1618–19. It might be argued that this intensified Calvinism, or High Calvinism, has far less to do with Calvin than it has to do with Beza. Beza's teachings, therefore, would prove to be hugely influential in the development in Arminius's own thought, both positively and negatively.

Early on, Arminius got along fine with Beza. It was actually with professor of philosophy Petrus Galesius, on the matter of logic, that Arminius had trouble. Arminius defended the positions of Ramus over and against the Aristotelian logic espoused by Galesius. The situation grew so uncomfortable that, for a time, Arminius and several of his classmates went to Basel to continue their studies. Exact dates are not known but it appears that Arminius was in Basel for roughly one year, between 1583 and 1584. While in Basel, Arminius was offered the title of Doctor on behalf of the university, an offer he respectfully declined, believing that he was not deserving of such a title at his young age. When he returned to Geneva, he took a milder approach, including less emphasis on his Ramist philosophy. In fact, while at Geneva, Arminius had very little discord with Beza at all. It might even be argued that at the time Arminius was a proud student of Beza's.

This is not to say that Arminius cheerfully endorsed Beza's views on predestination, for such is not evident. The opposite, though, is also not evident. Keith Stanglin and Thomas McCall believe, "It is just as likely that Arminius, as an heir of the early Dutch Reformation, always held to a sort of conditional predestination."[7] What is clear is that Arminius thought fondly of Beza, Beza believed Arminius to be an apt student, and that Arminius certainly learned Beza's theology while in Geneva. There is evidence of other students who strongly objected to Beza's thinking, but it cannot be proved that Arminius was in that camp during his early days as a student at Geneva.

Arminius's studies in Geneva came to an end in 1586, followed by a short trip to Italy with his good friend Adrian Junius. This trip to Rome stands as a mysterious transition in Arminius's life. Critics have made up all sorts of elaborate stories about Arminius's activity in Italy, most of which involved consorting with Roman Catholics—even the Pope himself. This is a difficult argument to maintain, though, as Arminius was consistent throughout his life in his criticism of the Roman Catholic Church in general, and popes in particular. In reality, we know that Arminius and Junius visited Padua and Rome. While in Padua, they listened to the lectures of the renowned philosopher Giacomo Zabarella and "Arminius himself gave lessons in logic to some German noblemen."[8] Before heading back to Holland, the two friends made a quick trip to Rome, where they did see Pope Sixtus V, though from a great distance. Not much else is known of this trip. Upon returning from Italy, Arminius stayed for a few months in Geneva, before assuming his

7. Stanglin and McCall, *Jacob Arminius*, 29.
8. Bangs, *Arminius*, 79.

post as a pastor in Amsterdam in 1587. Whatever happened on their travels, it is clear that when he returned and began his pastorate in Amsterdam, he was at odds with the stringent and intensified Calvinism of Beza and most of the Reformed Church.

FOR DISCUSSION

1. Arminius's early years were lived in a world torn apart by religious and political strife and violence—between Roman Catholics and Protestants in particular. In 1575, his hometown of Oudewater was destroyed, it's inhabitants slaughtered, by forces fighting for Spanish Catholics in search of Protestant converts to punish. How might this religious landscape have affected Arminius's life and theology?

2. What are some basic elements of the *via media* between Roman Catholicism and Protestantism traversed by Jacob Arminius?

3. Why was Arminius fond of Theodore Beza? What parts of Beza's teachings was he critical of?

Chapter 3

ARMINIUS'S PASTORAL CAREER

AFTER PASSING HIS MINISTERIAL preparatory exams in 1587, and thus proving his aptitude to begin ministry, Arminius officially began his work as a pastor in early 1588. He was ordained in the same year at the Old Church in Amsterdam, where Arminius would go on to serve for fifteen years. Arminius's pastoral assignment placed him in a rapidly growing and changing urban center. In particular, the city was experiencing rapid economic development, which, coupled with the strong theological arguments of the day, resulted in a dynamic setting for life and ministry. All accounts reveal that Arminius fully embraced his role as pastor, and was even elected secretary of the *classis*, or local ministerial council, in 1589.[1]

In addition to his duties as a pastor, Arminius's early days in Amsterdam were also taken up with the courtship of his future wife, Lijsbet Reael, the daughter of city councilman Laurens Jacobsz. The two were married on August 25, 1590. Unfortunately, though we have every reason to think that Jacob and Lijsbet had a happy marriage, Arminius left

1. Bangs, *Arminius*, 129.

no endearing letters or journal entries to give clear insight into their married life. It is clear, though, that in marrying Lijsbet the orphaned man from Oudewater now inherited a large and powerful family—a family at the very heart of civic life in Amsterdam. The couple lived in a house that was provided by the church, which in turn paid the city for its use. Their home, like the homes of so many other Protestant pastors of the day, was in a former cloister. As is the case with their marriage, there are no extant records of what home life was like for Jacob and Lijsbet.

From the very beginning of his ministry in Amsterdam, Arminius found himself in the middle of tension. He was careful and intentional to preach against the rising philosophy of humanism on the one hand, and also against the rigid Calvinism that was continuing to develop on the other. Such Calvinism tended to be split between sublapsarianism, or the belief that God's decree that select individuals would be saved came logically after the fall, and supralapsarianism, or the belief that God decreed some for salvation even prior to the fall. As we will see later, Arminius, though clearly a follower of Calvin, was not willing to affirm either of these two options. Likewise, he rejected the elevated status of humanity presented by the humanists as free from sin, or at least from its ongoing effects. Instead, Arminius believed that "our salvation rests on Christ alone and that we obtain faith for the forgiveness of sins and the renewing of life only through the grace of the Holy Spirit."[2] For Arminius, all people are sinners, and yet all people have the very real possibility of salvation by grace through faith. More than anything else, Arminius was a pastor, and he was concerned about preaching God's grace to his parishioners.

From the very beginning of his ministry in Amsterdam, then, Arminius found himself to be in a degree of

2. Quoted in ibid., 140.

tension with the *classis*, as well as with the teachings of his youth. Though he was to have a long and fruitful ministry, it was also to be marked by continual debate. Petrus Plancius, member of the *classis*, was the source of much of Arminius's early scrutiny. In particular, he criticized Arminius for his view on Romans 9, for undervaluing good works, and for his weak angelolatry—specifically that angels were not immortal. Regarding Romans 9, Plancius faulted Arminius for his view that children would be spared damnation if they were to die as children. Beza and the other high Calvinists believed, on the contrary, that every person was condemned on account of sin, regardless of their age. Fortunately for Arminius, his relationship with the town's leaders, the Burgomasters, was much better than with the clergy.

From the very outset of their marriage, Jacob and Lijsbet's home grew more and more full, and thus became busier and busier for Arminius. Lijsbet gave birth to their first child, a boy named Harmen, in 1591. Unfortunately, Harmen lived only a few weeks. He was buried in the Old Church. By the end of their time in Amsterdam, Aminius and Lisjbet had five living children. Several more died as infants. Lisjbet seemed particularly struck by tragedy, as many of her children and extended family members died long before she would, including her parents, who were both dead by 1602.

Over time, the conflicts died down and Arminius grew more and more trusted and involved in the ecclesial and civic life of the city. He led reforms in the city's Latin schools that lasted for centuries, helped guide and shape issues of morality in the city, served as secretary for the *classis*, and often represented the city in regional and national church gatherings. In fact, it is quite clear that Arminius became one of the foremost church leaders in Amsterdam and all of Holland. Bangs points out that Arminius actually had no conflict at all with his colleagues between 1593 and 1603, even getting along with his highly Reformed colleagues such as Plancius.[3]

In his later years in Amsterdam, the South Holland Synod tasked Arminius with writing a refutation of the theology of the Anabaptists. Interestingly, though Arminius agreed to the project, he failed to complete it. In fact, he doesn't appear to have attempted the project at all. It is probably the case that while Arminius was no Anabaptist, he was closer to their views on grace, predestination, and free will than he was to his Calvinist peers. It is most likely the case that this project actually stoked the growing fire of discord between Arminius and the strong Calvinism of the Reformed Church in which he ministered. It is soon after this uncompleted task, after all, that the conflict would heat back up for Arminius on the issue of his theology of predestination.

Amidst his theological and ecclesial work, Arminius, like everyone else, experienced the realities of everyday life. As we have seen, he and Lijsbet experienced the painful loss of several children. This had to take a toll on Arminius's ministry. The positive aspect of parenting must also be pointed out, as raising young children can be both a trial and a delight! Amidst all of this, Amsterdam was ravaged by the bubonic plague in 1601. It is reported that as many as 20,000 people died in what was Amsterdam's worst bout with the plague. As was always the case, the poorer areas of the city felt the effects worse than the wealthier areas. Arminius was actively involved in the care of those affected by the plague, often risking his own health to do so. He seemed to believe that God had called him to minister to the city, and that God would protect him while at the work of ministry. It should be pointed out, though, that while Arminius

3. Ibid., 159.

was actively engaged in service to those that were afflicted with the plague, his theological treatments of the plague were not nearly as helpful. Like others of his day, Arminius believed the plague to be a divine punishment for sin and unfaithfulness. Those who were spared, accordingly, were spared due to prayer, faith, and holy living. While it must be admitted that Scripture can certainly prompt such a view, it is equally the case that such a view does not fit so well with the graceful, benevolent God of Scripture. In particular, Arminius's own theology of grace does not seem to mesh well with such a view. Such is one of the constructive arguments of this book—that Arminian theology provides a far more faithful and rich account of theodicy than does highly Reformed theology. Thus, while Arminius cannot simply be let off the proverbial hook for his theological treatment of the plague, perhaps he might receive some pardon for having not fully fleshed out his theology yet and also for being a product of his day and age. Nonetheless, one would hope that Arminius would have approached the terrors of the plague with the sort of robust theology of grace that characterized so much of his work.

Near the end of his tenure in Amsterdam there were some clear signs that Arminius was ready to make a full-time jump into the academy. First, as his ministry went on in Amsterdam, Arminius became increasingly concerned with writing and publishing his works. Second, Bangs and Caspar Brandt both point out that, during the plague, Arminius had two documented encounters with people who were wrestling with assurance of their salvation.[4] It might be argued that such issues helped prompt him to revisit issues that he had not dealt with much since his days as a student—specifically those areas where he found increasing

4. Ibid., 174; and Brandt, *The Life of Arminius*, 74.

dissonance with the Reformed tradition.[5] Both Bangs and Brandt seem to indicate that these two encounters, and there were likely others, served as a prompt of sorts for Arminius to turn his focus from pastoral to more academic concerns. Specifically, he focused on issues of grace, predestination, and free will—issues that repeatedly caused him to feel at odds with the theology of the Reformed Church.

Thirdly, Amsterdam underwent a radical change at the turn of the sixteenth century. At this time, Amsterdam became a hub for global trade, shipping in particular. As such, the power dynamics of the city changed drastically. The change in the city's power brokers brought with it the embrace of the rigid Calvinism with which Arminius was at odds. Moreover, this change also brought a heightened embrace for the cause of war with Spanish Catholics.

Finally, Arminius's later years in Amsterdam were spent wrestling with the Epistle to the Romans, chapters 7–9 in particular, as well as with Englishman William Perkins's controversial pamphlet on predestination. His work on Romans 7, and especially chapter 9, forced Arminius to deal with the issue of predestination head on. In this work, Arminius sides with controversial former priest Gellius Snecanus, as well as Augustine, and comes out clearly in opposition to his former teacher Beza. For Arminius, Romans 9 is about justification by faith—which is always preceded and assisted by grace. As such, it affirms predestination. But what type of predestination? For Arminius the answer was the predestination of those who have faith in Christ. In this way, Arminius is fully Reformed. Human action does not result in or merit salvation for Arminius. It is also not the case, though, that God decides prior to creation who will be saved and who will be damned according to Arminius.

5. Both Bangs and Brandt seem to indicate that these encounters were of particular importance for Arminius.

Such is the teaching of Beza and of Calvinism afterwards. Instead, Arminius opts for a more complicated, middle-of-the-road sort of position. He uses the terminology of vessels, saying that humans are created as vessels for God's grace and goodness. As a result of the fall, however, we must choose what type of vessel we will be: open or closed, mercy or wrath. Humans do not choose, and thus affect, salvation, but we do have a say in whether or not we are open to God. If we are open to God, then grace can transform a sinner's heart into a vessel of mercy fit unto salvation, according to Arminius. If we are hardened and closed off to God, though, then we obviously cannot be gifted salvation. Salvation is not the result of human choice, therefore, though there is a degree of choice involved. Arminius notes that Beza, on the other hand, believes that human agency has no place in the matter, and that God hardens us by God's irresistible will.[6] As we will see later, this, for Arminius, makes God the author of evil—something that is detestable to Arminius. Arminius was convinced that Beza, and the Calvinists that followed him, were completely wrong in their interpretation of Paul on this matter, and he was determined to correct this. As a result, he again came under fire from local clergy.

If his treatment of Romans 7 and 9 did not land Arminius in enough hot water, his *Examination of Perkin's Pamphlet* surely did. William Perkins was a British Puritan, who was a professor of moral theology at Cambridge. He died in 1602, just prior to the completion of Arminius's examination of his work, which was completed in the same year. Bangs calls him, "the first important English theologian since the Reformation."[7] His book, or pamphlet, was

6. Arminius, *The Works of Arminus*, 3:509 (hereafter Arminius, *Works*).

7. Bangs, *Arminius*, 207.

published in 1598 and again in 1599 due to its popularity. Perkins's topic was predestination, which he hoped to present in a more preferable way than did Calvin. In reality, though, he ended up articulating the sort of supralapsarianism found in Beza and Calvin's other prominent followers of the day.

Central to Arminius's examination is his view that biblical predestination has a christological framework. That is, predestination concerns humans as sinners, and is determined through Christ.[8] Predestination is neither theoretical nor abstract. It has nothing to do with a divine decree prior to creation, and everything to do with God's graceful response to human sin. Looking to Ephesians, Arminius says that predestination is thoroughly christological and involves our adoption as children [of God], redemption through the blood of Christ, the forgiveness of sins, and the revelation of the mystery of the divine will.[9] Arminius is certain that this is the biblical "definition" of predestination, over and against the more theoretical rendering of the position articulated by the likes of Perkins and Beza and others. Arminius spends over 200 pages fleshing out this important difference! Interestingly, William Nichols suggests that Perkins's beliefs on predestination remained, primarily, an academic affair and were not preached from the pulpit.[10] This is strikingly opposite from Arminius's approach as a pastor and his concern: the salvation and wellbeing of his parishioners. Arminius's primary concern, then, is pastoral, while his primary starting point is christological. His opponents, on the other hand, have primarily academic concerns, which are derived from logical or philosophical starting points. While they use much of the same terminology it

8. Arminius, *Works*, 3:274–75.

9. Ibid., 275.

10. William Nichols, in Arminius, *Works*, 3:251.

must be seen that they were, essentially, speaking entirely different languages. This will be strikingly evident in Arminius's great *Declaration of Sentiments*, written in 1608.

It is surely the case that these academic endeavors caused Arminius to desire the university setting, but also, and perhaps more importantly, to feel called to focus the remainder of his life on the articulation and defense of his theological positions, none of which was more important than his view of predestination. Arminius could no longer keep quiet about his displeasure with the direction that Reformed theology was headed. He was increasingly moved to engage with his theological and ecclesial opponents in word and in writing. As a result, the relative peace he had worked for in Amsterdam was crumbling and conflict loomed. For all of these reasons, a move to the university was immanent.

FOR DISCUSSION

1. Arminius's ministry in Holland is characterized as walking a line between two different prominent views in tension with one another. What are these two views? How is Arminius's position within the tension important?

2. How was Arminius's response to the effects of the plague of 1601 inconsistent with his larger body of teachings and the direction in which his teachings lead?

3. Arminius drew sharp criticism for his interpretation of Romans 7–9. What might be some interpretive differences between the way so-called "rigid Calvinists" and Arminians would interpret these passages?

Chapter 4

ARMINIUS'S ACADEMIC CAREER

THE EFFECTS OF THE plague were far-reaching, and had effects upon Arminius's life that extended beyond the realm of pastoral care. In particular, both Lucas Trelcatius, who was a professor of theology at Leiden, and Arminius's good friend and fellow Amsterdam pastor, Franciscus Junius, succumbed to the plague in 1602. Trelcatius's death opened up a position at the University of Leiden that eventually would be filled by Arminius. Almost immediately upon Trelcatius's death, friends of Arminius began to write letters and have conversations with influential people, urging the appointment of Arminius as Trelcatius's replacement. Opponents of Arminius did the same, but with very different hopes for Trelcatius's successor. Eventually, school leaders agreed to offer the position to Arminius. This proved to be only a minor step in the process, though, as Amsterdam's burgomasters needed to release Arminius from his commitment to the Amsterdam church. The process of acquiring permission for Arminius's release also provided the opportunity for Arminius's critics to voice their concerns about Arminius's theology. As a result, a series of public meetings ensued that involved not only tense discussions about Arminius's employment, but also the orthodoxy of his theological teachings. Finally, in May of 1603, all sides came to agreement, and Arminius was officially released from assignment in Amsterdam and appointed as professor of theology at Leiden. Arminius and Lijsbet, who was nine months pregnant, along with their five children under the age of ten, moved to Leiden in June 1603. Arminius then began teaching later that autumn.

The entirety of Arminius's time in Leiden was marked by conflict. In particular, there was strong tension between Arminius and his colleague from the theology faculty Franciscus Gomarus. Gomarus, a fellow Dutchman, was a strong proponent of the rigid Calvinism of Beza and others. Additionally, Arminius battled with illness throughout most of his time in Leiden.

Arminius's first order of business upon assuming his duties at Leiden was to present himself for doctoral examination. This process involved a formal examination as well as a public disputation. The former, interestingly, was conducted by Gomarus, who would forever regret having approved Arminius. The latter was given at a public academic convocation and was on the topic of the "Priesthood of Christ." Arminius was successful on both accounts and publically awarded the title of Doctor on July 11, 1603. Arminius then fully gave himself to his work. His time was well occupied with lessons, writing, and public disputations. Furthermore, whatever hesitancy Arminius previously had about publically articulating his positions, now appeared to be gone. Issues of predestination, election, atonement, and proper biblical exegesis regarding such doctrines received central focus for Arminius. He was determined to put forth more biblically faithful and theologically sound articulations of these important doctrines than those of his rigidly Reformed counterparts. Such resilience gained him many friends as well as many enemies. Arminius's years in Leiden were, therefore, quite difficult.

Eventually, in 1608 the High Court of Holland requested that Arminius and Gomarus present written statements about their theological disagreements to the National Synod later that year. They would also be asked to present and defend their positions in person in front of the same Synod. According to Bangs, this was, in effect, "an inquisition."[1] The result of this request is a work that is Arminius's most important and has had the most lasting influence: *The Declaration of Sentiments*. Perhaps most importantly, in this work he provides clear definitions of what his supralapsarian (Gomarus) opponents believe, and why this is a corruption of Scripture. He then provides his position on such matters, and defends why they are biblical and supported by Christian tradition, the great councils of the church in particular. Leaving a more thorough investigation of the *Declaration of Sentiments* to chapters 6 and 7, it is important at least to note that Arminius states that predestination is not the central doctrine to the Christian faith, and that it is only biblical if it is grounded in Christology (which is the central tenet of Christian faith) and if it results in salvation for all those who believe. *The Declaration of Sentiments* is a powerful document and, in many ways, it provides a thorough summary of Arminius's theology.

Unfortunately, Arminius was unable to make it through all the meetings with the Synod and Gomarus. In fact, having left early, he died peacefully at home with his wife, children, and some friends on October 19, 1609. Tuberculosis proved to be an unbeatable foe. He was buried on October 22 in the Pieterskerk near his home in Leiden. Family, friends, and opponents alike gathered to pay their respect to one whom all would agree was a good and

1. Bangs, *Arminius*, 307.

faithful Christian man and pastor. Arminius's good friend Junius, who gave the oration at the funeral, said this about his friend, "[T]here lived in Holland a man whom they who did not know could not sufficiently esteem, whom they who did not esteem had never sufficiently known."[2] Fitting words indeed for such an important, polarizing, and passionate follower of Christ.

Having looked, albeit briefly, at the life of Arminius, it now remains to examine his theology. With his biography as a backdrop, therefore, we shall examine a few of Arminius's most important theological arguments. That Arminius was a man from humble roots must always be remembered. Having lost his father at a young age, he was dependent upon a series of benefactors for his care and education. As a teen he lost the remainder of his immediate family in the battle of Oudewater. Moreover, Arminius's familiarity with suffering did not end with adolescence. He experienced the premature death of several of his own children, lived through the plague, and battled with tuberculosis himself for several years before dying at a young age. Arminius knew suffering. Such events would surely always remain with him. Furthermore, despite his academic training, he was a pastor. He spent fifteen years in the pulpit and showed remarkable ability to convey difficult concepts to everyday people. As a pastor, he was first and foremost a student of Scripture. He loved Scripture and sought to share with others the love of the God revealed in Jesus Christ as witnessed to in Scripture. Arminius the man, in other words, should not—and indeed cannot—be separated from Arminius's theology. As lofty and scholastic as it was, Arminius's theology was both biblical and practical. For that reason, engaging Arminius's theology is just as stimulating and beneficial today as it was in the seventeenth century.

2. Quoted in ibid., 331.

FOR DISCUSSION

1. What is the name of the work produced by Arminius in response to the formal request for a public accounting of the disagreements between Arminius and Gomarus? What are some key elements of this work as stated in this chapter?

2. How do Junius's words at Arminius's funeral foreshadow the future reception and impact of Arminius's teachings?

PART 2

ARMINIUS'S THEOLOGY

Chapter 5

INTERPRETATION OF SCRIPTURE

As the early Church developed and spread out, it became increasingly necessary to teach new leaders to read and interpret Scripture faithfully. This need went hand in hand with the early Christian pursuit of orthodoxy, and the subsequent christological and Trinitarian controversies of the third and fourth centuries. It was important, in short, for Christians to be able to affirm essential core doctrines, and as a result to identify those teachings that were less than biblical. I would argue that the church's purpose behind this was to positively identify herself and her core beliefs. A resulting effect, though, was the identification and excommunication of heretics, or those who pushed the faith in directions that were skewed and out of line with the teachings of Scripture. Essential to this entire process was the interpretation of Scripture.

Throughout the patristic and medieval periods, exegesis, or the interpretation of Scripture, was dominated by what we now refer to as the fourfold sense of Scripture. This view affirms that Scripture is both written down, and therefore fixed, and yet also living and active. In short, this view assumes a supernatural and prescientific worldview, one that is not commonly held today. The fourfold sense of Scripture allowed for various levels of meaning of Scripture. Exegetes, therefore, were presented with hermeneutical options when interpreting and teaching Scripture. These levels of meaning are as follows: (I) literal, (II) allegorical, (III) tropological or moral, and (IV) anagogical, or the spiritual or heavenly reading of Scripture. To the spiritually mature, multiple levels of meaning could be found in most biblical passages. Spiritual maturity is key for this view, as it assumed that only those called and equipped, both spiritually and academically, could access the various levels of meaning within Scripture. As a result the tropological and in particular the anagogical interpretations of Scripture were elevated by many above the literal and historical senses. Biblical interpretation was after all a priestly function. This worked very well in a day and age without the printing press, let alone bookstores, computers, and the internet! Such a position can easily be critiqued, however. Perhaps it is important to remember one crucial benefit to this manner of biblical interpretation: it assumed and required faith as the lens through which to read and interpret Scripture. The hope was that biblical interpreters were those of faith and humility who read and interpreted Scripture to grow in spiritual maturity, for the purposes of leading others in the same. Spiritual guidance—something like the *Rule* of St. Benedict, for example—was intended to guide the process of biblical interpretation. This ensured that those who interpreted Scripture did so faithfully, reverently, and prayerfully.

The fourfold sense of Scripture allowed for some really beautiful and faithful exegetical work, and this approach is still important for many today. Well-intentioned as it was, though, the fourfold sense of Scripture allowed for various kinds of mistreatments and misunderstandings about the nature and function of Scripture. Primarily, it allowed for corruption by those in power. After all, it was the priest and the priest alone, who read and interpreted Scripture for his congregation. This beautiful and problematic understanding of Scripture held sway for almost 1,000 years. Many factors led to its demise, none more powerful, though, than the invention of the printing press and the subsequent translation and printing of the Bible into various languages. This process made Scripture accessible and understandable to common people. It was not long after Gutenberg's invention of the printing press in Germany that Martin Luther posted his famous ninety-five theses on the church door in Wittenberg challenging church authority, biblical interpretation, and basic Christian doctrine. The ensuing Reformation was characterized by the phrases *sola Scriptura* (Scripture alone) and *sola fidei* (or salvation by faith alone—as testified to in Scripture). The Reformers, Luther and Calvin in particular, believed that a literal and historical reading and interpretation of Scripture was best, and that such a reading would result in the understanding that salvation comes by grace through faith, period. The Reformers yearned for a simplification of the Christian faith, one that was less corrupted by longstanding ecclesial practices, one that was more concerned with individual faith.

It must be pointed out, though, that the Reformers did not simply want Scripture alone, for they assumed a whole system of Christian doctrine as central to biblical interpretation. Things like the divine attributes and the divine decrees, as well as the basic understanding that God is Triune, the hypostatic union (the doctrine of the two natures of Christ), as well as the resurrection were central, dominant categories through which Scripture was read and interpreted. In other words, biblical interpretation in the scholastic and Reformation periods still assumed that the reader and interpreter were beginning from a position of orthodox

Christian faith. Biblical interpretation was a practice that began in faith, and drove one toward even deeper faith. One of the best examples of this way of reading Scripture can be found in Augustine's *On Christian Doctrine*, which teaches young pastors how to read, interpret, and teach Scripture. There, Augustine instructs pastors that they must approach Scripture from a fundamental and doxological (worship) position of belief in the Trinitarian God who was revealed in Jesus who is fully God and fully human, and who was raised on the third day. Just as can be said positively about the fourfold sense of Scripture, biblical interpretation begins in faith, assumes faith, and enhances and deepens faith, all for the purpose of *doxa*, which is worship or praise. It would be many years before interpreters would begin from a basic position of scientific rationalism and therefore skepticism, as many do today.

Arminius inherited and embraced a scholastic and Reformed view of Scripture. As such, Arminius's biblical interpretation has several key characteristics: he held firmly to the classical divine attributes, read Scripture in a literal sense, employed a christologically focused hermeneutic, and relied upon the church's classical interpretation of Scripture, as outlined by the church councils, when he believed that Scripture was not entirely clear. Arminius approached Scripture with these presuppositions, with the clear understanding that Scripture was meant to edify, instruct, and produce faith in the reader, as well as in the church as a whole. Furthermore, as has recently been pointed out by Jeremy Bangs, Arminius was heavily influenced by Philosopher Jacomo Zabarella.[1] Recall that one of Arminius's and Junius's primary reasons for travelling to Italy in 1586 was to hear lectures from Zabarella in his hometown of Padua.

1. J. Bangs, "Beyond Luther, Beyond Calvin, Beyond Arminius," in *Reconsidering Arminius*, ed. Stanglin, Bilby, and Mann, 57–87.

Bangs points out that Zabarella believed that there were two hermeneutical methods that led to truth: composition and resolution. Composition, according to Zabarella, involved utilizing a demonstrative argument that moved from general principles to particular effects. This was the common method of metaphysics and, therefore, theology as well. Resolution, on the other hand, works in reverse by moving from practical effects to general principles. When the results of these two logical systems coincide, clear confirmation occurs as to the truth of what was in question.

Arminius was not alone in his fondness for Zabarella's method; it was quite appealing to the Protestant scholastics. The logic on display in Zabarella's method is heavily focused upon practical demonstration and usefulness. As it applies to Scripture, the results of biblical interpretation should be applicable personally and practically. Even metaphysics, it would seem, would have a very simple and practical application for Zabarella. Zabarella's framework, therefore, should be helpful to us in understanding Arminius's exegesis of Scripture.

First, as already noted, Arminius approached Scripture in a way quite similar to most other Protestant Scholastics. He affirmed the classical divine attributes, including: (God's) unity, love, truth, goodness, beauty, omnipresence, omnipotence, omniscience, simplicity, infinity, immutability, and impassibility. The last two, in particular, along with God's omniscience, are most important here. Arminius assumes God's immutability and impassibility—that God does not change or suffer. This logical point of departure safeguards God's trustworthiness and difference from created beings, all of which are subject to time and decay, and goes hand in hand with things like eternality and aseity. Most Christians, aside from those who affirm process theology and/or open theism, assume these things as well, though probably not as blatantly as did scholastic theologians. By affirming God's immutability and impassibility, Arminius affirmed that God is other than creation, outside of time, space, and the general physical laws of the created order. Likewise God's utter sovereignty is affirmed, as God is not *necessarily* affected by creation. It is possible to argue that God is *voluntarily* affected by creation, only not out of necessity. My belief is that such can be done while remaining faithful to Arminius's theology. Anything else, though, moves beyond the positions set forth by Arminius himself.

Affirming God's omniscience moves us into the debates that will be examined in chapter 7, and thus will only briefly be dealt with here. In sum, to affirm God's omniscience is to affirm God's divine, and therefore perfect, knowledge. "God knows all things," it might be said. Arminius is not interested in affirming anything but this, in terms of God's knowledge. What that means, however, is up for debate. For some, omniscience entails God perfectly knowing all future events and choices. For others, God knows which possible choices an individual can make in any given situation. God does not know exactly what will happen, but always what might happen depending upon the situation. This position is often called "middle knowledge." Still others claim that God knows the entire range of possible choices for each and every event and knows the general direction things will move in but does not know which specific choices will be made in specific instances.

This issue is further complicated by the impact that God's omniscience might have upon human freedom. For example, if God knows what I will do before I do it, am I really free to make a choice? Does God's knowledge of the future cause our actions, therefore, or can God know what we will do, or even what we might do, without impacting our ability to choose? How one answers these questions typically drives them toward either a version of free will or else determinism (each with many different "flavors"). Some attempt to navigate this admittedly difficult terrain through modified positions such as God's middle knowledge (or Molinism—that God knows not only what one will choose but what one *would* choose). Or, they try to hold both systems together in what is often known as compatibilism (that human free will and determinism are compatible). Arminius is often accused of these latter two because he completely affirmed God's sovereignty, and yet also affirmed human freedom. As will be seen in chapter 7, though, human freedom for Arminius is always predicated upon God's grace. Thus, as many have argued, human will is perhaps best thought of as "freed will" rather than free will.[2] Humans, sinners as we are, simply cannot choose grace on our own—and it is certainly not owed to us, as other medieval and scholastic theologians would argue. But, despite the crippling disease of sin, Arminius affirms that we are able to choose—we are free—and thus we are responsible.

As I understand it, Arminius believes that humans are vessels. We are broken and sinful, through and through, but we remain vessels. By God's ever-present grace, we are able to choose to be open to God or closed to God. Thus, we can reject God or else we can be open to God. If the latter occurs, then God's grace fills, cleanses, redeems, saves, and sanctifies us. I would argue, therefore, that Arminius believes that we can choose evil and reject God, or we can choose to be open to God. God will then do the rest, meaning that we are not responsible for our own salvation. The line between Arminius and Calvin, and the latter's Reformed progeny, is thus very thin indeed. There does remain always, though, a line of difference.

2. Thanks to Mark Mann for our many emails and conversations on this subject.

Returning to Arminius's interpretation of Scripture, the divine attributes, along with all their "baggage," are ever present to Arminius. Undoubtedly, this approach smacks as almost offensive to many modern/postmodern readers. It might be argued that assuming such things prior to reading Scripture will result in the interpreter finding exactly what they already assume. The answer is "yes and no." Yes, interpreters who assume the divine attributes are likely to find them in Scripture. But perhaps having such open assumptions allows one to honestly engage in self-critique and thus to have their positions challenged. It is also true, though, that beginning with such positions places a heavy burden on the positions, a burden which they may, therefore, be unable to carry. In this way beginning with the divine attributes may cause one to eventually move away from them. Additionally, postmodern critics have pointed out that we all have agendas and presuppositions. The Enlightenment belief in the disinterested reader/interpreter has been debunked. We are all firmly entrenched in our own various cultural biases and presuppositions. Perhaps it is more helpful to be honest about this, as those like Arminius were, than to pretend that one is interpreting Scripture in an unbiased manner.

Second, Arminius reads Scripture in a primarily literal sense. In his *Private Disputations*, for example, as elsewhere, Arminius emphasizes the perspicuity of Scripture.[3] Its meaning and intention, in other words, are fairly simple, accessible, and understandable. While Arminius does talk about Scripture's various levels of meaning he clearly prefers the literal, or practical reading of Scripture. Here, he demonstrates the influence of Zabarella, and also indicates that some parts of Scripture are very difficult to understand. His belief, though, is that those parts that pertain to salvation

3. Arminius, *Private Disputations* VIII and IX, in *Works*, 2:327–30.

are plain and clear. Still, for Arminius there are various levels of meaning to Scripture, and learned study is advised to faithfully interpret and teach it. The basic meaning of Scripture regarding the nature of God and how we might be saved is, however, clearly understandable in a literal sense.

Third, Arminius's method of biblical interpretation was christologically driven. Arminius is often described as a theologian of grace. This is indeed an apt description. It must be remembered, though, that Arminius's understanding of grace is, quite specifically, the grace of God the Father, made possible by the atoning sacrifice of the Son, available to us by the Holy Spirit. Arminius's doctrine of grace is not grounded in creation, but rather in redemption, in the salvific work of the Son, Jesus Christ. The same could, of course, be argued for all of Arminius's theology, election and predestination in particular.

Arminius believed that the Holy Spirit actively works through Scripture, pointing readers and listeners (the church) toward knowledge and faith in the Son, who is the full revelation of the Triune Godhead. He believed that Christ could be seen in the Old Testament, and that it is not only helpful but faithful to read the Old Testament through the lens of Jesus, and thus in light of the life, death, resurrection, and ascension of Jesus. There is a clearly defined agenda to Scripture, in other words, for Arminius. That agenda is to point us toward the God the Father, through Jesus Christ the Son, by the dynamic power of the Holy Spirit. While there are all sorts of other aspects to Scripture, such as moral teaching, guidance toward wisdom, and historical accounting, the christological sense to Scripture was key for Arminius.

Finally, while Arminius affirmed the divine inspiration of Scripture, he was also willing to admit that the meaning of Scripture is not always clear. Such instances, were, for the most part, issues of linguistic and cultural translation, and did not pertain to the essentials of salvation. In such instances, he believed it helpful to refer back to the church's historical interpretation of such verses and passages. This included, especially, church councils. While humans certainly err, Arminius believed that the Holy Spirit was not only at work in Scripture, but also in the community of believers across time. Arminius was of the opinion that the church's classical interpretation of difficult passages was not canonically binding, but was usually quite helpful.

Arminius went so far as to attribute perfection to Scripture. What he meant by perfection, however, was very different than the way the term is usually employed today. The perfection of Scripture, for Arminius, lies in its ability to reveal Christ to us, as well as salvation. Scripture is perfectly inspired, he would argue. I would suggest, therefore, that Arminius's view of the perfection of Scripture is quite similar to the view commonly called "plenary inspiration," which is held by groups such as the Church of the Nazarene. According to plenary inspiration, Scripture perfectly and inherently reveals to us all things necessary for salvation. In short, Scripture perfectly accomplishes its task, which is to narrate the story of God and to teach us how to be saved. It does this perfectly, despite all the while containing imperfections of various sorts, such as misspellings, mistranslations, misunderstandings, and even contradictions. Arminius would thus attribute perfection to Scripture but not to the church's translation of Scripture. That said, he viewed the church's translation of Scripture as significant, weighty, and authoritative.

In summary, then, we would do well to remember that when reading and interpreting Scripture, Arminius held firmly to the classical divine attributes, read Scripture in a literal sense, employed a christologically focused hermeneutic, and relied upon the church's classical interpretation of Scripture, especially that of the church councils, when he believed that Scripture was not entirely clear. All of this was important because Arminius was, first and foremost, a pastor. Arminius's pastoral calling and convictions must always be kept in mind, but especially when understanding how he read and interpreted Scripture. Arminius took his pastoral duties seriously. He cared about his congregants, and especially about their salvation. He believed it was his duty to ensure that they all knew about Christ Jesus, his sacrifice for them, and, as a result, the free gift of grace made possible for them by the Holy Spirit. Arminius interpreted Scripture in a way that he thought people would understand and accept. This pastoral impulse, especially as it pertains to Scripture, was evident in his writings, and it is a huge part of his lasting legacy today. With this in mind, we will now examine the core of Arminius's theology: his understanding of Christology and of the Trinity.

For Discussion

1. What is the fourfold sense of Scripture, so prominent in medieval exegesis in particular? What are some strengths and drawbacks of this hermeneutical approach to Scripture?

2. What are some important elements of the teachings of the Philosopher Jacomo Zabarella? How were these influential on Arminius?

3. A distinction is suggested between "free will" and "freed will." What is this distinction? Is it helpful in understanding Arminius's thought, especially as contrasted with Reformed theology in general, or rigid-Calvinism in particular?

Chapter 6

CHRISTOLOGY AND TRINITY

CHRISTOLOGY IS THE PRIMARY doctrine for the church to
attend to if she is to be faithful. In particular the church
must wrestle with the two natures of Christ, who we affirm
to be fully divine and yet also fully human without admix-
ture or change. In affirming this doctrine, which we now call
the hypostatic union (of the two natures of Jesus), we open
ourselves up to the question of polytheism. In other words,
do we worship one God or two (or three)? If we are to be
faithful to Scripture, then we must affirm monotheism, or
the worship of One God. But clearly this understanding of
monotheism adheres to anything but a textbook definition
of the term. For if we affirm the divinity of Christ how can
we hold on to monotheism? It is clear that a faithful answer
to these questions requires faith as well as unconventional
logic, to say the least. It is usually the case that wrestling
with Christology has driven the church toward a Triune understanding of the Godhead. Such was the case for the early
centuries of the church. Two of the greatest examples of this
type of wrestling, and the Trinitarian theology that ensues,
can be found in Augustine's *de Trinitate* and Basil's *On the
Holy Spirit*.[1] Each argues for a fundamental unity amidst

1. Interestingly, though one is from the "West" and one from the
"East," they both end up saying roughly the same thing about the Trinity.

distinction, as well as a true difference assumed within the
unity of the Triune Godhead. "This is anything but easy,"
they would both say, "speaking about the unspeakable."
And yet as followers of Christ that is precisely what we are
called to do. We must speak about the unspeakable. Doing so, I would suggest, should ultimately be done within,
and should drive us toward, doxology or praise. The same
sort of logic is on display in Arminius's theology as well.
We must begin, therefore, with his doctrine of Christology,
followed closely by his Trinitarian theology.

At the center of Arminius's theology, holding it all together, was his doctrine of God, specifically Christology and
his theology of the Trinity. Christology is the object of theology, for Arminius, and it was the object of Scripture as well.

> Since we have God and his Christ for the object of our Christian Theology . . . For God has
> unfolded in Christ every one of his blessings.
> *'For it pleased the Father, that in Him should all
> fulness [sic] dwell;' (Col. i,19)* and that the *'fulness of the Godhead should dwell in him,'* not by
> adumbration or according to the shadow, but
> *'bodily.'* For this reason he is called, *'the image of
> the invisible God;' (Col. i.15) 'the brightness of his
> Father's glory, and the express image of his person,'
> (Heb. i,3)* in whom the Father condescends to
> afford to us his infinite majesty, his immeasurable goodness, mercy and philanthropy, to be
> contemplated, beheld, and to be touched and
> felt; even as Christ himself says to Philip, *'He
> that hath seen me, hath seen the Father.' (John
> xiv, 9.)* For those things which lay hidden and
> indiscernible within the Father, like the fine
> and deep traces in an engraved seal, stand out,
> become prominent, and may be most clearly
> and distinctly seen in Christ, as in an exact and

> protuberant impression, formed by the applica-
> tion of a deeply engraved seal on the substance
> to be impressed.[2]

For Arminius, Jesus is truly the full revelation of the Godhead. He is that which makes clear and comprehensible the hidden and indiscernible within the Father. Christ is God laid bare, revealed, and opened up for all of creation to see. He is redemption, healing, new life, and, most importantly, salvation. In this way, Arminius is fully in line with the early church fathers, and especially the Reformers. In fact, it is here that the profoundly Reformed nature of Arminius's theology is so clearly visible, for he seeks to interpret all things in light of the revelation of God in Christ. Here Arminius is being faithful to the Reformation cry of *sola Scriptura*. He embraces the principles of the Reformation in such a way that he is more interested in fidelity to Scripture than to supporting the Reformed "tradition." It might even be argued that Arminius's theology is more christologically focused than Calvin's, and certainly than Calvin's followers, but less than Luther's. Whether or not one affirms this claim, it must be affirmed that Arminius's Christology is a splendid example of post-Reformation christologically-focused theology.

Arminius's treatments of Jesus often focus on his "offices," which are commonly termed the priestly, prophetic,

---

2. Arminius, *Oration I*, in *Works*, 1:272. To be fair, Arminius states that God is the primary object of the Christian religion and that Jesus Christ is the secondary object. That said, while the two can be distinguished they cannot be separated. After all, Jesus is the revelation of God and is what and how we know the Father. Such is evident in the above quote. I would argue that when Arminius distinguishes between the primary and secondary objects of theology, he is doing something similar to Basil who states that, "if we might count, we do *not* add, increasing from one to many," so that $1 + 1 + 1 = 1$. Basil, *On the Holy Spirit*, 72. Thus, the God revealed in Jesus, to whom Scripture points us, is the object of theology for Arminius.

and the kingly. Just as there are three persons within the one divine Godhead, so Jesus has three roles or offices.

In his collection of private disputations, Arminius places Christ's priestly office prior to his prophetic one, which is a reversal of the common order of the offices of Christ. There does not appear to be any real intentionality behind this reversal, other than simply having a high view of the priestly office. Arminius does not intend to downplay the office of the prophet, in other words, but simply to elevate the office of the priest. Under this office, Arminius places Jesus's role as the savior and mediator of humanity. He is our savior in that his blood was spilled as a sin offering (despite being free from sin), effectively paying the price for all those who were subject to sin and death. Jesus thus takes sin into himself, freeing humanity from its bonds, cleansing us, and ultimately destroying its power over us. In doing so, he is our mediator with the Father, for where the Father used to see only the stain or nothingness of sin, he is now able to see the pure sacrificial love of Jesus, and the beginning of the restoration of creation. Christ's work as savior cleanses, makes whole, redeems, and even makes holy creatures that were otherwise completely given over to sin. Arminius describes Christ's priestly role here as being highly eucharistic in nature, for he is broken and poured out, in order to heal and restore. He is quick to point out, though, that this is not an ongoing, earthly offering. Thus it does not take place in the (Roman Catholic) mass, but rather in heaven as an offering given directly to the Father on our behalf.

The prophetic office of Christ, for Arminius, is divided into Christ's prophetic role on earth and the activity of the risen Christ who sits at the right hand of God the Father almighty. Jesus was sanctified and made ready for the former office in his baptism. The descent of the Holy Spirit and the voice of the Father confirm this. It was in this office that

Christ resisted the temptations of the devil and the principalities and powers. For Arminius, Jesus fulfills his prophetic office in three ways: in his bold teachings, holy living, and the end to which the former two brought him. That he was martyred or killed for insurrection by those who should have accepted him only solidifies his role as prophet.

Jesus not only held the offices of prophet and priest, but also of king. His kingly or regal office is characterized by the fact that all things were created by and through him. Most importantly, his sacrificial death and subsequent defeat of humanity's most ancient foes—sin and death—result in his being Lord of all things. Christ's roles as king are as follows for Arminius. First, he offers sinful humans the vocation and calling of participation in the kingdom of God, without this they and we cannot belong to God's kingdom. The opposite is also true, and will be seen in his final role. Christ's kingly role also involves legislation, in that he assigns and calls his followers to particular tasks or duties. Furthermore, he gives blessings and also punishments in this life, in proportion to that which is to come. Finally, his is the final judgment. As the one who took upon himself our rightful punishment, our ultimate fate is in his hands.

For Arminius, as is the case with so many other theologians across time, Christ Jesus, our crucified and risen Lord, is priest, prophet, and king. He is so neither by adoption nor because he is identical with the Father, but because he is the Son of God, the second person of the Holy Trinity, the perfect revelation of God, in whom the fullness of God was pleased to dwell. Arminius, therefore, held to a very high Christology. Everything, even predestination and election, was dependent upon Jesus for Arminius. This difference will be central to the debates with those who sought to intensify Calvinism on the matter of predestination.

As strong, as high, and as central as his Christology was, though, Arminius was clear not to collapse the Trinity in upon itself by equating the Father with the Son. In fact, he utterly rejected the term *autotheos* or "very God," a term that Calvin and much of the Reformation embraced. Arminius's rejection of this term is tricky, to say the least. Understanding why ushers us into a brief discussion of Arminius's Trinitarian theology. For Arminius, the key to his rejection of the term *autotheos* is seen in his clarifying statement, "so far as it [*autotheos*] signifies that the Son of God has the Divine Essence *from himself.*"[3] Arminius does not dispute that Jesus is verily God. Rather, Arminius disputes that Jesus derives his divine essence from himself, or that he is God in isolation from the Father as well as the Spirit. As the Nicene Creed states, Jesus is "God from God, light from light, true God from true God [or very God from very God], begotten not made, of one being with the Father, . . ." Jesus is true God, or very God, and he is certainly complete and whole, but he is also this amidst the fundamental relationality of the Holy Trinity. Arminius is clear to affirm, no matter how high his Christology might be, that Jesus's true divinity is, nonetheless, derivative of the Father by the power of the Holy Spirit. Arminius further expands upon this discussion in his *Apology against Thirty-One Theological Articles*. There, he continues to reject the term *autotheos* for Jesus and also for the Holy Spirit. With the church fathers, he claims the term can only be applied to the Father, who is first among equals within the Holy Trinity. It is appropriate to say, therefore, that, while the Trinity cannot be separated, and is defined by distinction amidst unity and unity amidst distinction, there is a preference or prioritization of the Father over the Son and Spirit. The Father truly is, therefore, first among equals within the Godhead. Arminius does actually go on, then, to claim a certain level of comfort with

---

3. Arminius, *Private Disputation* XXXV, in *Works,* 2:380; italics mine.

the term *autotheos*, provided that it is used to refer to Jesus as God, so long as it is remembered that Jesus as the Son derives his divine essence from the Father. In his rejection of *autotheos*, then, it should be clear just how strong an emphasis Arminius places upon Trinitarian theology.

Arminius also has a very high view of the Holy Spirit, one that certainly reveals his Trinitarian theology. For example, Arminius is always sure to follow the Trinitarian pattern and discuss the divinity of the Holy Spirit, when discussing the Father and the Son. Moreover, in like fashion to his argument regarding Jesus, Arminius rejects the term *autotheos* for the Holy Spirit, for the Spirit—like the Son—is complete and yet also derivative of the Father and the Son. Arminius posits that the Holy Spirit is, properly understood, a person proceeding from the Father and the Son. While not being *autotheos*, the third person of the Holy Trinity, according to Arminius, is distinct, divine, infinite, eternal, illimitable, and utterly and completely holy. Moreover, he says that "he is the person by whom God the Father and the Son perform all things in heaven and earth, and that He is not only Holy in himself, but likewise the Sanctifier of all things which are in any way holy and so called."[4] Arminius also suggests that while we must attempt to do so, we cannot ultimately define the Holy Spirit but only describe the Holy Spirit.[5] Arminius attempts to do just that in his public disputation on the Holy Spirit and ends up confessing that

> [t]he Holy Ghost is of the same Divinity with the Father and the Son, and is truly distinguished by the name of God. For He who is not a creature, and yet has a real subsistence, must be God; and

4. Arminius, *Public Disputation* VI, in *Works,* 145.

5. This claim is strikingly similar to Anselm's "proof" of God's existence, which he thought to be a description rather than what we think of today as a proof or definition.

> He who is from God, and who proceeds from
> the Father, not by an external emanation, nor by
> a creation performed through the intervention
> of any other Divine Power, but by an internal
> emanation.[6]

Finally, it must be pointed out that Arminius's understanding of the Holy Spirit as one of the three persons of the Holy Trinity is based upon the witness of Scripture. From Old Testament to the New, he sees the Spirit of God as present and active and derives his Trinitarian understanding from the reconciliation of the Holy Spirit's role in Scripture to that of the Father and of the Son.

Simply put, Trinitarian theology is the assumed framework for Arminius's theology. That God is anything other than Triune is completely unthinkable to him. This much is overwhelmingly evident in his work. Arminius sums up his Trinitarian theology best in saying,

> This doctrine of the sacred and undivided
> Trinity contains a mystery which far surpasses
> every human and angelical understanding, if it
> be considered according to the internal union
> which subsists between the Father, the Son, and
> the Holy Ghost, and according to the relation
> among them of origin and procession. But if
> regard be had to that economy and dispensation
> by which the Father and the Son, and both of
> them through the Holy Spirit, accomplish our
> salvation; the contemplation is one of admirable
> sweetness, and produces in the hearts of believ-
> ers the most exuberant fruits of Faith, Hope,
> Charity, Confidence, Fear, and Obedience, to
> the praise of God the Creator, the Son the Re-
> deemer, and of the Holy Ghost the Sanctifier.—
> May "the love of God the Father, the Grace of

6. Arminius, *Public Disputation* VI, in *Works*, 2:148–49.

the Lord Jesus Christ, and the Communion of
the Holy Ghost, be with us," and with all saints.
Amen! (2 Cor. Xiii,14.)[7]

While it is not the case that Arminius puts forth lengthy
sustained arguments for the Trinity, it is the case that he simply assumes the Triunity of the Godhead. For Arminius, the
God who is revealed in Jesus of Nazareth, the God who appeared to Moses in the burning bush, the God of Abraham,
Isaac, and Jacob, is the Triune God. Jesus reveals to humanity
the fullness of the love and relationality of the Godhead, but
he is not the same as that relationship. He is God's love and
reconciliation revealed. We can know him, because the Holy
Spirit preveniently guides us toward him. Because we know
him, we not only know the Father, but know the Father as
our Father. Christ Jesus, then, is the point of contact and connection with the Triune God, and as such he is the invitation
to humanity to participate in the life and love of the Triune
God. Arminius not only thought this, but he believed this
and he faithfully proclaimed it throughout his entire career
as both a pastor and a professor. His Christology, and therefore his Trinitarian theology, was the foundation for all of his
theological work, which included, most especially, his understanding of grace, election, and predestination.

7. Ibid., 149.

FOR DISCUSSION

1. How did the classical understanding of the two natures of Christ lead to the understanding of God as Triune in the early Church? How did these doctrines develop, while still affirming monotheism?

2. How is Jesus priest, prophet, and king? How is the understanding of these three "offices" of Christ important and helpful?

3. Why does Arminius insist on rejecting the term *autotheos* as applied to Jesus? What is his concern? Is this an important article of his theology worth holding on to, or not?

Chapter 7

GRACE, PREDESTINATION, AND ELECTION

> O Thou, wha in the heavens dost dwell,
> Wha, as it pleases best Thysel',
> Sends ane to heaven and ten to hell,
> A' for Thy glory,
> And no for onie guid or ill
> They've done afore Thee![1]

HAVING EXAMINED ARMINIUS'S DOCTRINE of Scripture, as well as his views on Christology and the Holy Trinity, the foundation has been laid to examine his most important and, indeed, controversial teachings regarding grace, predestination, and election. It is here, more than any other place, that Arminius left his mark upon the church. Arminius refused to embrace the common Reformed understanding of predestination and election espoused by so many and championed by Francisco Gomarus and Theodore Beza in particular. Arminius refused to embrace this position, in short, because he held to a very strong doctrine of

---

1. Excerpt taken from "Holly Willie's Prayer," by Robert Burns, cited in Harrison, *The Beginnings of Arminianism*, 14.

grace and refused to allow God to become the "author of evil," as he would put it. His refusal was nothing short of revolutionary, and ended up paving the way for a large contingency of Protestant Christians to do the same. Heirs to Arminius's theological teachings are quite numerous still to this day, though few know much about the great man from Oudewater anymore. In his strong rejection of the particular brand of intensified Calvinism that would eventually be championed by the Synod of Dort, Arminius paved a new way. Though he was most definitely not a papist, Arminius's understanding of grace, and therefore his views of predestination and election, moved him closer, perhaps, to Roman Catholicism than to traditional Reformed Protestantism. Ultimately he would remain a Reformed Protestant, but in a way that I would describe as a *via media*, or middle of the road, figure. The issues of predestination and election were so important to Arminius that he risked everything—his career, his legacy, and his livelihood—to defend his fundamental impulse, namely, that all are elect in Christ, and thus have the real possibility of salvation. God does not will that anyone should perish and be damned, according to Arminius. Arminius staked his entire theology on this position. To see this argument in its most complete form, we are well served to look to Arminius's *Declaration of Sentiments*.

During the years Arminius served as a Pastor in Amsterdam, he was able to remain relatively low-key. After his somewhat reluctant acceptance of an invitation to leave his parish and assume the role of Professor of Divinity at Leiden, however, he was never again able to keep out of public scrutiny. From the beginning of his professorship, Arminius was criticized and attacked by a vast array of theological opponents. Arminius tried to handle his critics in as polite and civil a manner as possible, trying hard to dodge public debates as often as possible. Finally, though, in 1608, just a year before his untimely death, Arminius acquiesced to the call for a formal defense of his position, especially on the subject of predestination and election, as compared to the views articulated by his colleague Gomarus. The result is his *Declaration of Sentiments*: his most powerful and systematic treatment of his various theological positions: predestination and election in particular. It was of course included in the Latin *Opera* of Arminius's works. It was also the first of Arminius's writings to be published in English.[2] *The Declaration of Sentiments* is Arminius's most significant, profound, and systematic work. It represents the mature Arminius, and should serve as a primer for all those who want to read and engage the work of Jacob Arminius.

In the *Declaration of Sentiments* Arminius discusses the providence of God, the free will of humanity, the perseverance of the saints, and the certainty of salvation, in addition to his main topic, predestination. In regard to the latter, this text offers Arminius's most systematic and yet concise treatment of the subject. He covers several different and popular ways of understanding and articulating predestination. In particular he addresses Gomarus's views, which he indicates are in line with the commonly espoused views of the "Supralapsarians."[3] In summarizing this position, Arminius states,

> That God has absolutely and precisely decreed to save certain particular men by his mercy or grace, but to condemn others by his justice: And

2. Bangs, *Arminius,* 307.

3. Calvin, for example, writes, "Predestination we call the eternal decree of God, by which He has determined in Himself, what He would have to become of every individual of mankind. For they are not all created with a similar destiny; but eternal life is foreordained for some and eternal death for others. Every man, therefore, being created for one or the other of these ends, we say he is predestinated either to life or death." Calvin, *Institutes* III.XXI.5.

to do all this without having any regard in such
decree to righteousness or sin, obedience or
disobedience, which could possibly exist on the
part of one class of men or the other.[4]

Accordingly, God simultaneously, prior to the fall—
prior even to creation—decided that some people would
be elect for salvation and that others would be destined for
damnation—and that a person could do nothing whatsoever to merit or change one's status as either elect or reprobate.
This position, as derived from Calvin, but especially his followers, and which takes its ultimate shape in the articles of
the Synod of Dort, represents an attempt to deal with some
very difficult passages of Scripture (Romans 8 for example).
This position also attempts to resist the heretical temptations of Pelgius's articulation of free will, through which human choice becomes the cause for salvation. For Gomarus,
and the "Supralapsarians," then, that which God foreknows,
God wills, and, thus, since God's fore-knowledge is complete, the result is a very limited understanding of freedom,
especially in regard to salvation or damnation.

Despite what critics might say, Arminius also has an
allergy to Pelagianism, as he absolutely does not want to
make salvation or damnation the meritorious effect to the
cause that is human choice. Or perhaps it is more accurate
to say that for Arminius damnation is most certainly the
direct and meritorious result of human choice—that choice
being sin. Salvation, on the other hand, is not earned but is
the result of the divine free gift of grace, whereby the human person can, effectively, choose God's ways over sin, not
through their own power but through the gracious power
of the Holy Spirit. In terms of salvation, then, the view of
human volition put forth by Arminius is one of confes-
sional receptivity and therefore participation. The same free

4. Arminius, *Works*, 1:550.

gift of grace is presented to all. Why only some choose to respond positively to grace is left to the realm of mystery. God fully knows, therefore, who will respond and choose God's ways, fully receiving grace, as well as those who will respond by choosing their own ways, thus receiving damnation. This knowledge, though, does not place a limitation upon humanity, effectively eliminating some choices from the realm of possibility. Arminius affirms all the classical characteristics of God (immutability, impassibility, aseity ...) and thus it is not a problem for God, who exists outside of time, to know what will transpire in the fullness of time, without willing or causing such events.[5]

Arminius proceeds to offer a rather systematic rejection of the doctrine of Predestination as articulated by the "Supralapsarians." It is safe to conclude that, for Arminius, this doctrine, understood in this way, is more harmful than any other erroneously conceived doctrine to the Gospel of Jesus Christ.[6] That being said, he does affirm predestination, as classically defined, and he sets forth to positively state why. In order to do so effectively he lays out four "absolute decrees of God," which will serve to frame not only his articulation of predestination but his theology as a whole.

God decreed to appoint for humanity, his Son, Jesus Christ, to be the "Mediator, Redeemer, Saviour, Priest, and King, who might destroy sin by his own death, and who might by his obedience obtain the salvation which had been lost, and might communicate it by his own virtue."

5. I would argue that it is precisely due to his affirmation of these categories of God's existence, as articulated by Thomas Aquinas and Augustine, for example, that Arminius is able to affirm God's complete and utter sovereignty and yet maintain a central position for free will. Human free will only becomes problematic when God is stripped of these classical categories.

6. Arminius's twenty-part rejection of Gomarus and the supralapsarians' view of predestination can be found in, *Works*, 1:554–75.

God "decreed to receive into favour those who repent and believe, and, in Christ, for HIS sake and through HIM, to effect the salvation of such penitents and believers as per-severed to the end; but to leave in sin and under wrath all impenitent persons and unbelievers, and to damn them as aliens from Christ."

God "decreed to administer in a sufficient and effica-cious manner the means which were necessary for repen-tance and faith; and to have such administration instituted (1) according to the Divine Wisdom, by which God knows what is proper and becoming both to his mercy and his se-verity, and (2) according to Divine Justice, by which He is prepared to adopt whatever his wisdom may prescribe and to put it in execution."

God "decreed to save and damn certain particular persons. This decree has its foundation in the foreknowl-edge of God, by which he knew from all eternity those indi-viduals who would, through his preventing grace, believe, and, through his subsequent grace would persevere,—ac-cording to the before-described administration of those means which are suitable and proper for conversion and faith; and, by which foreknowledge, he likewise knew those who would not believe and persevere."[7]

First, and most importantly, then, God the Father eternally appointed his Son to take on flesh and as such be for humanity mediator, redeemer, savior, priest, and king. Thus God communicated salvation by means of his own virtue, and not that of humanity. Through the efficacy of the redeeming and reconciling work of Christ Jesus, God likewise committed to accepting into salvation those who would believe and have faith in Jesus. Conversely, God committed to allow those who would not believe and have

7. Ibid., 589–90. All capitalization, punctuation, and other stylis-tic oddities are quotations from the original author.

faith in Jesus to have the necessary ends of their own self-destructive will—eternal perdition.[8] Thirdly, to those who desire it, God determined to provide all that is necessary to achieve true faith and repentance—the result of which is salvation. Finally, Arminius maintained that God's divine foreknowledge does not result in determinism and, therefore, that, while God's eternal foreknowledge includes knowledge of all those that will be saved as well as all those that will be damned, it does not guide, force, or fate any person into either salvation or damnation.[9]

Though the language is indeed tricky and the logic can be confusing, Arminius's point should be clear: God created all creatures to enjoy God's goodness and grace and as such to receive salvation. Because of human free will, which may in fact be humanity's chief and most distinguishing

8. It seems clear to me that the destructive end awaiting many—however it be understood—is for Arminius a human creation and thus not a place created by God specifically as a place to house and torment the damned. Obviously, God must allow such a place to exist, but its existence, as such, must be understood as the necessary end of human free will. Whatever hell is, therefore, it is other than God; it is as God-free a place as can be conceived of, though if it exists at all, it obviously does so by God's grace, for existence cannot be attributed to a thing (or place) apart from God.

9. In stating these four absolute decrees of God, especially as they pertain to predestination, in such a way, Arminius reads very similar to Thomas, who says of predestination: "Predestination most certainly and infallibly takes effect; yet it does not impose any necessity, so that, namely, its effect should take place from necessity . . . but not all things subject to providence are necessary; some things happening from contingency, according to the nature of the proximate causes, which divine providence has ordained for such effects . . . *moreover all that has been said about the divine knowledge and will must also be taken into consideration; since they do not destroy contingency in things, although they themselves are most certain and infallible.*" Thomas Aquinas, *Summa Theologica* I.1, q.23, a.6 (trans. Fathers of the English Dominican Province, 130).

characteristic, however, humanity was able to and in fact did choose to reject God and God's grace. Sin and death are the resulting merits of humanity's utilization of its free will. Knowing humans would reject God, God nonetheless created humanity, and in the fullness of time ordained to send God's own Son to overcome sin and death, and thus rebuild the bridge between God and creation that sin had destroyed. Finally, though God's grace is extended to all, only some will choose to respond affirmatively, while many others will respond negatively. Salvation is thus not earned by humanity and damnation is not the divinely appointed end of anything. God creates all for the purposes of salvation. All those who receive salvation, receive it based solely upon God's goodness. Those who do not receive salvation receive their just reward and the natural end for that which they chose to worship rather than God.

The anchor that holds Arminius's entire system together, the thing that truly does distinguish his theology from the theology of, say, Pelagius, is his christological foundation for predestination: election.[10] Notice that the

10. Arminius notes that, for example, Augustine addresses this very issue as a stark point of contrast between his own theology and that of Pelagius. Arminius affirms Augustine's position as being the accurate one of the two, and he casts his lot, therefore, along with Augustine, as opposed to Pelagius. "Besides this, the same Christian Father [Augustine] says, 'Let Pelagius confess, *that it is possible for man to be without sin*, in no other way than *by the grace of Christ*, and we will be at peace with each other.'—The opinion of Pelagius appeared to St. Augustine to be this,—'that man could fulfill the law of God' by *his own strength and ability;* but with still greater facility *by means of the grace of Christ.*' I have already most abundantly stated the great distance at which I stand from such a sentiment; in addition to which I now declare, that I account this sentiment of Pelagius to be heretical, and diametrically opposed to theses words of Christ, '*Without me ye can do nothing:*' (John xv, 5.) It is likewise very destructive, and inflicts a most grievous wound on the glory of Christ." Arminius, *Works,* 1:619–25.

first "Principle Head" of the doctrine of predestination for the so-called "Supralapsarians," at least according to Arminius, is,

> That God has absolutely and precisely decreed to save certain particular men by his mercy or grace, but to condemn others by his justice. And to do all of this without having any regard in such decree to righteousness or sin, obedience or disobedience, which could possibly exist on the part of one class of men or the other.[11]

Thus for this group, according to Arminius, the divine categories of mercy and justice take foundational precedence in understanding predestination. Arminius agrees that predestination should not be founded upon anything other than God's pure goodness. Likewise, he agrees that salvation is not a derivative of human actions. The fundamental difference, though, is that Arminius's starting point is not God's mercy and justice, abstractly defined, but the concrete expression of God's mercy and love—indeed of all that God is—in the person of Jesus Christ.[12] In fact, Arminius does not refer to God's mercy and justice until article III of his "Absolute Decrees of God," making it quite clear that election for salvation, and therefore predestination as a whole, is based solely upon God's grace as fully and perfectly revealed in Christ Jesus. Moreover, in point seventeen of his twenty-part rejection of predestination as articulated

11. Ibid., 554.

12. A similar point can be seen in Arminius's preference of Christ as the *fundamentum electionis*—that Christ is the author, procurer, and executioner of our election—versus the understanding of Christ as the *fundamentum electorum*—the first of the elect, the foundation of the elect (but not of election itself). Arminius clearly sides with the former, along with Martinius of Breme, as opposed to, for example, Gomarus. Ibid., 449.

by Gomarus and the "Supralapsarians," Arminius states rather strongly that said doctrine actually "inverts the order of the Gospel," in that it places God's alleged absolute will to "bestow salvation on certain particular men, and . . . to give those very individuals repentance and faith, by means of an irresistible force, because it was his will and pleasure to save them" prior to God's most fundamental will, which is to save (or at least to offer salvation to) all of creation through the mediating, atoning, and reconciling work of the Son, Christ Jesus.[13] This causes Arminius to go on by vigorously stating that this understanding is not only contrary to the gospel, but that it stands in open hostility to the gospel! Christ alone must be the foundation for election, and thus for predestination, or else these doctrines have no place in faithful Christian theology—and Arminius does affirm that they have a very significant place.

So Arminius makes his case for the errors and dead-ends of the "Supralapsarian" or the intensification of Calvin's understanding of predestination, and therefore, election. Arminius's interlocutor is not Calvin but rather his theological progeny, such as Theodore Beza and Francisco Gomarus.[14] Their theology can best be seen in the "system"

13. Ibid., 508–9.

14. When will those who stand in the so-called "Wesleyan-Arminian Tradition" finally begin to study, and even embrace, the theology of John Calvin? After all, both Arminius and Wesley seemed to be not only fond of Calvin's theology, but to be intentionally in agreement with the vast majority of Calvin's teachings. Recall Wesley's statement that he differs from Calvin on only a "hair's breadth" (Wesley, "Letter to John Newton"). Likewise, in discussing justification, Arminius states, "[N]one of our divines blames Calvin, or considers him to be heterodox on this point; yet my opinion is not so widely different from his as to prevent me from employing the signature of my own hand in subscribing to those things which he has delivered on this subject, in the Third Book of his *Institutes*; this I am prepared to do at any time, and to give them my full approval"

of theology that would be articulated by the Synod of Dort a decade after Arminius's death. I would argue that the rigid system that stems from Dort, with its five points, though obviously derivative of Calvin, deserves to be treated as something quite different from the actual theology of Calvin. Arminius describes the former quite well, and makes his disagreements abundantly clear. Of Calvin himself, though, he has less to object to.

God, in God's very divine simplicity, who alone is absolute perfection, and who as such alone possesses aseity, eternality, immutability, and impassibility, and the other attributes, elects all of humanity, in Christ, to salvation, thus restoring the breach caused by sin. God's perfect foreknowledge, though, allots that God knows whether or not individuals will respond in faith to God's grace. As a result, Arminius maintained predestination as the non-deterministic knowledge and plan that some will receive eternal beatitude, while others will receive, by their own choice, eternal perdition. The cause, moreover, that effects either of these two ends is not to be found in human volition, but rather in the Son, Christ Jesus, who is God's eternal author, procurer, and executioner of election. This cause, by the aid of the Holy Spirit, allows humanity to freely choose God's grace and salvation, and especially to reject it: choosing instead humanity's own path, which ends in destruction. God thus provides the very means to choose either God or that which is other than, and thus contrary to, God.

God's grace is truly supreme for Arminius. Of course, the same might be said for many other theologians as well, but it must be said of Arminius. Specifically, Arminius understands God's grace in light of the death and resurrection of Jesus. As the Apostle Paul wrote in Romans 5:8, "[W]hile we were still sinners, Christ died for us." He died not for the

---

(Arminius, *Works*, 2:636).

righteous, nor only for the few. He died for the elect, which, understood christologically, would be all of humanity, for all time. Election does not equal salvation, but it does equal grace. All are elect in Christ, for Arminius. As such all are the recipients of grace, and are given the ability to respond positively to God, as well as to reject God. Interestingly, to be able to reject God, then, requires God's grace. In this way Arminius's entire theological system is dependent upon his understanding of grace. In Christ Jesus all persons are elect. All are predestined by him, in him, and through him to be eligible for salvation. Salvation will be forced on no one, but it is God's will for everyone. In the end, God's grace is the source of salvation, and not our works. For Arminius, God's grace allows a person to freely respond positively to God by opening up to God. Likewise, though, God's grace enables a person to reject God, walking away from the very source of grace, in favor of what can only be understood to be falsity and bondage. Salvation and damnation, then, are properly understood as reliant upon God's grace. Yet this grace is not based in logic, or in eternal principles, but primarily in the person and work of Jesus, and secondarily in our response to the revelation of God in Christ Jesus.

FOR DISCUSSION

1. What are classic and contemporary examples of theological positions that make God the "author of evil?"

2. Is God's sovereignty challenged by human freedom? Why or why not?

3. Compare and contrast positives that might come from the positions of both the "supralapsarians" and of Arminius, in in regard to predestination. Theologically speaking, what is lost and what is gained by each position?

PART 3

ARMINIAN THEOLOGY TODAY

Chapter 8

ARMINIUS ≠ PELAGIUS

HAVING EXAMINED THE LIFE and theology of Jacob Arminius, it remains to discuss his legacy today, present as it is in the theological sensibility known as Arminianism. Along the way we will examine Arminius's thought in correlation with three important theological figures. The first figure, the notorious early church heretic Pelagius, is one whose theology is often conflated with Arminius's. I will argue, however, that this could not be a worse move. Secondly, we will examine the critical appropriation of Arminius's theology by the Church of England's most famous reformer, John Wesley. I will argue that Wesley is, indeed, a faithful Arminian, and that he was so quite intentionally. Finally, we will examine what similarities might lie between the great twentieth-century Protestant theologian Karl Barth and Arminius. This last pairing might be seen to be the most unlikely of all. I believe, however, that there are many similarities between these two Reformed reformers, the most important of which are their doctrines of election and predestination. Finally, we will conclude with a look at what it means to be an Arminian today.

It has already been demonstrated that Arminius's theology gave way to a theological sensibility bearing his name.

This sensibility, or movement, often served as a caricature for a theological outlook characterized by libertarian free will and works righteousness. For many, especially after the Synod of Dort, Arminianism represented a theological system wherein humanity retained the *imago Dei* or image of God, despite the fall. This allowed humanity to do good on its own and even to choose God—effectively earning salvation. For some, Arminianism even entailed a view of humanity that was so positive and optimistic as to teach that humanity was owed grace and, ultimately, salvation. Basically Arminianism has meant, for many, a view of humanity that is so positive and optimistic that God is barely needed, if at all. This understanding of Arminianism is surely a caricature. No serious or even casual reader of Arminius's works could affirm that this, indeed, represents Arminius's teachings. Rather, this view of Arminianism resulted from the steady, powerful attacks of Arminius's critics, Gomarus and Beza in particular. Unfortunately, this caricaturization was made all the more easy by Arminius's untimely death.

Another root cause for this caricature of Arminius's thought comes from his unfortunate, but all too common, grouping with the heretical theologian Pelagius. Pelagius too has been made into a caricature; he is a symbol for the humanistic perversion of Christianity. Pelagian Christianity is heavy on grace while being light on judgment, or so it is often claimed. Since the fifth century, the church has opposed Pelagianism wherever it has been found. Sometimes, though, in the process of critique we end up vilifying a person or way of thinking that is not fully understood yet. This may or may not be the case with many of the various parties accused of Pelagianism or semi-pelagianism over the years. For the purpose of this work, we will assume Pelagius's own teachings and Pelagianism to be roughly identical. It is probably safe to assume that, as with Arminius and

Arminianism, this is not necessarily true. Be that as it may, the view of Pelagius and Pelagianism, whether an accurate or a caricatured description, is the heaviest and most consistent critique levied against Arminius and Arminianism. For the purposes of this chapter, then, the picture of Pelagianism painted by critics, especially those intensely Reformed critics of Arminius's day, will be examined. Arminius's teachings will be cross-referenced against these teachings.

Most of the works of Pelagius have not survived. Of that which has survived, his commentary on the Epistle to the Romans is most important.[1] This work demonstrates Pelagius's theology in a way that both affirms and challenges the common perception of Pelagius the heretic. Perhaps the most concise and helpful summary of what has come to be known as Pelagianism comes from Pelagius's close friend and student Caelestius. Caelestius was heavily influenced by Pelagius, and his teachings were commonly grouped together with Pelagius's. These teachings, as identified and condemned by the Synod of Carthage (411), are as follows:

- Even if Adam had not sinned, he would have died.

- Adam's sin harmed only himself, and not the human race as a whole.

- Children just born are in the same state as Adam before the fall.

- The whole human race neither dies through Adam's sin or death, nor rises again through the resurrection of Christ.

- The Mosaic Law is as good a guide to heaven as the gospel.

- Even before the advent of Christ there were men who were without sin.

1. De Bruyn, trans., *Pelagius's Commentary on St. Paul's Epistle to the Romans*.

The rejection of these theses by the Synod of Carthage, along with the unwavering critiques of St. Augustine, helped pave the way for the eventual rejection of Pelagius's works, and Pelagianism as a whole, by the Council of Carthage in 418. Afterward, though Pelagianism had been rejected, the prevalence of Pelagius's thought remained. Eventually it blossomed again in what is commonly called semi-pelagianism, which is a position that seeks to have the best of both Augustinian and Pelagian impulses. In short, semi-pelagianism attempts to stay in line with Augustine's teachings of original sin, but in such a way that human nature is not completely corrupted. As a result, humanity retains free will, though not in terms of the maturation of faith into salvation. Semi-pelagianism teaches that there is just enough goodness inherent still in humanity, that it is owed grace (at least some grace) and that humanity can, as a result, choose God on its own, without the need of supernatural grace.

Having so thoroughly worked to combat Pelagianism, Augustine also attacked semi-pelagianism, which would ultimately be condemned at the Council of Orange in 529. As is the case with all such teachings, however, Pelagianism and semi-pelagianism continue to have influence to this day. Some would argue that they were heavily influential in the medieval and scholastic debates regarding pure nature, and again in the advent of Protestantism. More importantly, after the early condemnation of each it became quite popular for one to label an opponent as either a "Pelagian" or a "semi-pelagian," effectively making each movement into a caricatured label one might be branded with simply for being different. As such, the gap between Pelagius's thought and Pelagianism (as well as semi-pelagianism) grew. The same has already been argued for Arminius's theology and Arminianism. The point is this: if one desires to be viewed as an orthodox Christian, one had best avoid the pitfalls of both Pelagianism and semi-pelagianism—regardless of whether or not these teachings are consistent with Pelagius's own theology. In what remains of this chapter, then, our task is to examine several of the primary tenets of Pelagianism, as outlined by the Synod of Carthage (411), asking whether or not Arminius was guilty of being a Pelagian. I would argue that it can quickly and easily be demonstrated that Arminius was neither a Pelagian nor a semi-pelagian, despite his emphasis on free, or possibly freed, will. To do so, I will utilize, primarily the public and private disputations, as well as his *Apology against Thirty-One Theological Articles*,[2] all found in the second volume of *The Collected Works of Arminius*.

Arminius begins his *Apology* by stating that he previously affirmed and continues to affirm that Scripture suggests that "believers under the Old Testament, before the ascension of Christ, were not in Heaven."[3] He adds, though, that such a discussion is really of no profit to the church at all. He says that Scripture is not perfectly clear about this, and that our knowledge of salvation, after Christ's ascension, is not reliant upon this whatsoever. With Augustine, he states, "I prefer doubting about secret things, to litigation about those which are uncertain."[4] This axiom is an important one to Arminius. Those who follow in his steps would do well to embrace such a position as well. Arminius believes, along with the majority of the early church, that those who lived and died prior to Christ's resurrection and ascension, go to someplace other than heaven proper. This other place might be a sub-level of heaven, purgatory, or a different place altogether. On this, Arminius accurately states that Scripture is not clear. Arminius's opinion is that, wherever the "place" that the immortal souls of those who died prior

2. Hereafter *Apology*.
3. *Apology*, in *Works*, 2:1.
4. Ibid., 2.

to the resurrection and ascension might go, it grew increasingly better and more glorious when Christ ascended into heaven. There they await the full consummation of God's kingdom, at which time they will be raised with Christ and all the saints into the full blessedness of his kingdom. In this argument, Arminius displays a clear respect for the power of the Old Testament, and yet a clear prioritization of the New Testament over the Old. It is thus safe to say that while Arminius had a high opinion for the Mosaic Law, he did not hold it to be as equal a guide unto salvation as the gospel.

Similarly, Arminius absolutely did not believe that there were those without sin prior to the advent of Christ. Simply put, Arminius strongly affirms the doctrine of original sin. Arminius does state that, properly speaking, Adam (and thus Eve as well) did not need faith, as they knew God directly and intimately. This makes their offense all the more heinous. Furthermore, their rebellion was real and not symbolic for Arminius. It broke God's law and violated God's trust. In doing so, Adam and Eve sought to supplant God's sovereignty with their own—thus birthing humanity's ceaseless and tragic striving after self-sovereignty. For all those after Adam and Eve, faith would be necessary. First this was a faith in God's law and ultimate will, and secondly it was faith specifically in God's Son, Jesus.

Everything truly did change with the sin of our first parents, according to Arminius.

> The whole of this sin, however, is not peculiar to our first parents, but is common to the entire race and to all their posterity, who, at the time when this sin was committed, were in their loins, and who have since descended from them by the natural mode of propagation, according to the primitive benediction: For in Adam "all have sinned." (Rom. V,12) Wherefore, whatever

punishment was brought down upon our first
parents, has likewise pervaded and yet pursues
all their posterity: So that all men "are by nature
the children of wrath," (Ephes. Ii,3) obnoxious
to condemnation, and to temporal as well as
to eternal death; they are also devoid of that
original righteousness and holiness. (Rom. V,
12,18,19.) With these evils they would remain
oppressed for ever, unless they were liberated by
Christ Jesus; to whom be glory for ever.[5]

It should be quite clear, therefore, that Arminius also
rejected the notion that Adam and Eve's sin harmed only
themselves. Instead, Arminius believed that the culpability
for that first sin affected, and continues to affect all people,
both biologically and socially. Not only do we inherit sin, in
other words, we also inherit a propensity and even a weakness toward it.

But what of children? Did Arminius believe that children are truly innocent, or did Adam's sin harm the entire
human race? In his *Apology* Arminius succinctly addresses
this very issue, even stating and distancing himself from
Pelagius/Pelagianism. Arminius is responding to theses attributed to Borrius, but which in this case ultimately stem
from Pelagius. It is suggested that these two believe that
infants who die, and who have not yet had the opportunity
to commit actual sin, will be saved, regardless of their faith
or the faith of their parents. The underlying premise to this
position is that original sin condemns no one, but only
actual (chosen) sins. The contrary position is suggested of
Augustine, and is touted as the "classic" view of (Christian)
"antiquity" by those with whom Arminius would seek to
disagree. In short, these opponents believe that all people,
including infants, who die having not made a personal

5. Arminius, *Public Disputation* VIII, in *Works,* 2:157.

confession of faith and having not been baptized will go to hell. In the case of infants, their damnation is predicated upon original sin. Arminius is not comfortable with this position. Instead, he cites the likes of Augustine, Prosper of Aquitaine, and his dear friend Francis Junius as not fully adhering to this so-called "classical" view.[6] According to Arminius, the primary reasons for their discomfort with the belief that children will not be saved upon their death is twofold. First, all believe that by grace baptism takes away the guilt of original sin. Second, Arminius points out that even those listed, such as Augustine, who say they believe that unbaptized infants will not go to heaven if they die prematurely, are not consistent about this. Such a position may have logical consistency in its favor, but it does not have grace. Arminius sides with Junius, who affirms that

> "all infants who are of the covenant and of election, are saved," but he also presumes, in charity, that "those infants whom God calls to himself, and timely removes out of this miserable vale of sins, are saved."[7]

For Arminius, as for Junius, God's grace is understood to be far greater than a logically consistent argument. Arminius believes the same is true for most of the church's greatest pastors and teachers. He concludes with a "What if?" question: What if an unbaptized child of an unbeliever is saved . . . could this really be said to occur apart from Christ and his direct intervention? Is this really too much to imagine? For Arminius it is not. Salvation is purely the result of the Father's grace, made possible by the Son's sacrifice, as witnessed to by the Holy Spirit. That God might save

6. It is extremely common of theology throughout history to strongly differ in one's understanding and interpretation of Augustine, with both "sides" using him against one another.

7. Quoted in *Apology*, 13.

an infant that has committed no sin is definitely within the realm of possibility for a loving, gracious, and all-powerful God. It must also be pointed out that if God elects to do so, it is surely not because salvation is owed, in any way, to any human, let alone an infant. Rather, salvation is the result of God's grace. It is God's hope for humanity, sinful as it is, and it is the hope of God that all might be saved.

Building upon this previous point, it would surely be ludicrous to ascribe to Arminius the view that Adam's death did not cause death for all people. Arminius is abundantly clear that he proudly affirms original sin. As we have seen, he does allow for God's grace to reach beyond the logic of the guilt of original sin, but such grace would be unlooked for and unlikely. Instead, we inherit the stain of original sin, and we also choose sin, voluntarily, as we grow older. Arminius is quite clear about this.

Arminius is even more clear about the fact that redemption is only possible through the resurrection of Christ Jesus. Here Arminius wants to be careful to avoid, among other things, universalism. He strongly affirms that salvation comes through Christ alone, and that Christ's meritorious death on the cross was undertaken with the redemption of all in mind. He does not want, however, to sound as if he believes that Christ's death will necessarily guarantee salvation for all. Again citing Prosper of Aquitaine, Arminius argues that the power and magnitude of Christ's sacrifice on the cross, his blood that was spilt, affected the whole world. This most important of sacrifices, then, made all people eligible for salvation. As such it was universal. That it results in the salvation of all, though, is not the opinion of Arminius. On this point, Arminius states that the controversy and confusion lies in the interpretation of his teachings, but not his teachings themselves, which he believes are straightforward. Thus it can be said that on this one point, or at least part of this one point, Arminius does affirm the position attributed to Pelagius as condemned by the Synod of Carthage. He does believe that the whole human race rises again through the resurrection of Christ. Yet for Arminius this is a christological and not an anthropological statement. The difference is huge indeed. As such, in regard to this classic tenet of Pelagianism, I cannot fault him for being a Pelagian whatsoever.

There remains one precept of so-called Pelagianism that must be sought out in Arminius's work. Was death a punishment or result of sin, or was it the case that had Adam and Eve not sinned they would still have died? Arminius's answer to this is quite clearly "No," they would not have died. In several places throughout his *Apology* and his public and private disputations, Arminius asserts double death to be a clear result of the first sin. In most cases, Arminius simply assumes that most are familiar with the concept of double death—that is, physical and eternal (or spiritual) death. This assertion, left unqualified, might lead some to question whether or not Arminius believed physical death to be natural even to our first parents—prior to the first sin. Any lack of clarity on this point, though, surely is satisfied in Arminius's private disputation 31, "On the Effects of the Sin of Our First Parents." In this disputation, Arminius claims that original sin has two main effects: offense [of God] and guilt. That latter, he argues, results in the entrance of, and slavery to, sin, as well as humanity's subjugation to death.

Regarding the punishment of death, Arminius states that it is twofold. First comes temporal death, which Arminius defines as the separation of the soul from the body. Second, humanity is subject to eternal or spiritual death, which is the separation of the entire person from God. Arminius goes on to parse out exactly how these are both punishments for sin, and thus were not original to creation.

> The indication of both these punishments was
> the ejection of our first parents out of Paradise.
> It was a token of *death temporal*; because Para-
> dise was a type and figure of the celestial abode,
> in which consummate and perfect bliss ever
> flourishes, with the translucent splendor of the
> Divine Majesty. It was also a token of *death eter-*
> *nal*; because in that garden was planted the tree
> of life, the fruit of which when eaten was suitable
> for continuing natural life to man without the
> intervention of death: This tree was both a sym-
> bol of the heavenly life of which man was bereft,
> and of the death eternal which was to follow.[8]

Able to eat, as they were, from the tree of life, Adam and
Eve clearly would have lived forever and thus not died. Death,
both physical and eternal or spiritual, then, is the direct result of, and a punishment for, original sin. This is abundantly
clear. The opposite cannot be argued of Arminius.

It simply cannot be argued that Arminius was a Pelagian. He was not. Arminius's teachings do not resemble in
any way the teachings that were rejected by the Synod of
Carthage (411). Arminius did, however, affirm that humanity has free will and is required to respond to God's grace, as
revealed in Christ Jesus by the power of the Holy Spirit. Unlike Pelagius, though, Arminius attributes even free will to
the grace of God. Some have argued, therefore, that human
free will, if it be understood in light of Arminius's teachings,
actually should be understood as freed will, for humanity
is only free in and through God's grace. I would agree that
this concept is indeed helpful in that while Arminius uses
the language of free will, he is always very clear to attribute
it to God's grace.

8. Arminius, *Private Disputation* XXXI, in *Works*, 2:374–75.

The question is, then, although Arminius is clearly not a Pelagian, was he a semi-pelagian? In short, a semi-pelagian is a person who affirms some, but not all, of Pelagius's heretical teachings. As demonstrated earlier, semi-pelagianism was also rejected by the early church at the Council of Orange (529). In his *Apology*, Arminius addresses this precise question. First, he cautions that "it would be quite easy, under the pretext of Pelagianism, to condemn all those things of which we do not approve, if we invent *[semi] half, quarter, three quarters, four fifths-Pelagianism*."[9] It takes more than a mild similarity to render one a Pelagian, after all. Arminius goes on to discuss two extreme opposites within Christianity, Pelagianism on the one hand, and Manicheism on the other. Manicheism espoused a very strong doctrine of dualism between good and evil, something that is quite foreign to the gospel message, the creation account in particular. Arminius suggests that faithful Christians would do well to chart a course directly in the middle of these two positions, in such as way as St. Augustine had done. Moreover, Arminius suggests that rather than labeling one a "Pelagian," it would be better to simply deal directly with the teachings and doctrines that seem troublesome as they are stated by the person in question. To do so allows the inquiry to remain solely on the topic of a particular person's teachings and not on the lingering shadow of Pelagianism—a term that, once said, surely taints the minds of both the interrogator and interrogated. Having engaged Arminius's teachings directly, I am satisfied that he was neither a Pelagian nor a semi-pelagian.

Finally, we must also remember, of course, that, though he was a heretic, Pelagius reached the decisions he did out of a desire to faithfully articulate Christian doctrine. As Jaroslav Pelikan has helpfully pointed out, most of the early heretics

9. Arminius, *Apology*, in *Works*, 2:56.

were not wholly off base but simply overemphasized one aspect of their understanding of the gospel to the detriment of the whole gospel. Thus in the case of Pelagius his desire to articulate a loving and creative God who endowed us with free will ended up making salvation a direct result of our belief—or even something that is owed to humanity. This is surely not the case. The church has rightly condemned Pelagius's teachings. But surely Pelagius's teachings were greater than just these. It must be the case that in most of his teaching he remained fairly orthodox, or he likely would not have drawn the attention he did for these teachings. There is surely more to Pelagius, then, than meets the eye. And as Arminius has suggested, we must be careful when throwing out blanket terms like "Pelagianism" or "semi-pelagianism" to describe someone's theological teachings. Doing so, especially in the case of a set of teachings that has been deemed heretical, imports all sorts of baggage into a discussion, most of which is unfair. Instead, we should seek to critically engage specific teachings and positions, holding them against Scripture and tradition for validity.

FOR DISCUSSION

1. What is so bad about Pelagianism? How has his thought been caricatured throughout Church history?

2. What is the difference between Pelagianism and semi-pelagianism? Is either applicable to Arminius's theology? Why or why not?

3. How is Arminius's understanding of human freedom based in Christology and not in anthropology?

Chapter 9

WESLEY THE FAITHFUL ARMINIAN

JOHN WESLEY WAS AN eighteenth-century religious reform-er within the Church of England. Wesley was well educated, attending the prestigious Charterhouse School followed by Christchurch, Oxford. In addition to his studies in Divin-ity, while at Oxford, Wesley became a Greek lecturer and a moderator of classes. He was also ordained in the Anglican Church during this time by the Bishop of Oxford. Wesley grew increasingly interested in piety and religious holiness. He was convinced that a pious holy life was central to fol-lowing Christ. In pursuit of such a life, he formed a group that would eventually become known, unaffectionately, as the "Methodists" due to their methodical way of living.

During a failed missionary attempt in Georgia (Unit-ed States), John Wesley became acquainted and enamoured with the Moravians, who placed strong emphasis upon church unity, piety, missions, and music. Eventually Wesley would critique the Moravians, but he would always be influ-enced by their distinct way of life and theology. Wesley re-turned to England from Georgia a frustrated and distraught young soul, uncertain of his calling or purpose in life. Then, in 1738, Wesley had an experience that would change his life forever. Shortly before 9pm, upon leaving an evening meeting on Aldersgate Street in London of a religious society that was reading the preface to Luther's commentary on the Epistle to the Romans, Wesley encountered God. Of that experience, he penned these now famous words,

> About a quarter before nine, while he was describing the change which God works in the heart through faith in Christ, I felt my heart strangely warmed: I felt I did trust in Christ, Christ alone for salvation; and an assurance was given me that he had taken away my sins, even mine, and saved me from the law of sin and death.[1]

Wesley would identify this as his conversion experience, saying that he was not really a Christian before this. Soon after, he began preaching the gospel and specifically the message of holiness to all who would listen. Sometimes Wesley, like fellow revivalist George Whitfield, would even preach in open-air fields to crowds of as large as 20,000. Wesley wanted personal and ecclesial reform—this message did not make established church leadership very happy. Eventually, as a result of the growing number of Methodist bands in the United States who lacked ordained pastors to administer the sacraments, Wesley ordained Thomas Coke. With this Wesley effectively, though very reluctantly, broke ties with the Church of England in favor of the newly established Methodist Episcopal Church. Wesley died on March 2, 1791. At the time of his death, he had 313 British preachers under his care and 76,968 members. He also was

---

1. Wesley, *A Plain Account of Christian Perfection,* 23.

responsible for 198 preachers in the United States, as well as 57,621 members.

Theologically, Wesley loved John Calvin and knew his theology quite well. He was also very familiar with Roman Catholic scholastic thought, and specifically the Aristotelian Thomism of the scholastic period. Wesley was equally well versed in the theology of the so-called "Eastern Fathers." Ultimately, though, Wesley preferred the theology of Arminius, especially on the issues of grace, predestination, and election.

Perhaps more than anything else, Wesley is known for being a great revivalist preacher, for his circuit-riding preaching, and for creating a system of worship and discipleship known as Methodism, which was structured around bands or small groups of intentional fellowship, accountability, and discipleship. Wesley's practical theology was thoroughly, consistently, and intentionally Arminian. That is to say, the shape and scope of his theology bears a clear resemblance to the theology of Arminius. Moreover, the fact that late in his life he began publishing a magazine entitled *The Arminian Magazine* speaks volumes. That said, Arminius's influence on Wesley is more implicit than it is explicit.

Some have argued that Wesley never read Arminius. Most, however, believe he was familiar with his works. If he did read Arminius's work, Wesley did not leave us a clear record of when and what. The question is, then, how did Wesley come to be familiar with Arminius's theology? It might have been as simple as an encounter with Dutch immigrants living and working in Lincolnshire, England, near where Wesley grew up. As Geoffrey F. Nuttall stated in his 1960 address to the Arminius Symposium in Holland, such a small issue may indeed be a large factor in the Arminianism of John Wesley. Nuttall notes that roughly 200 Dutch families migrated to the vicinity of Epworth, in

Lincolnshire, England. Under the leadership of Cornelius Vermuyden, they took up the task of draining around 60,000 acres of swampland. "It is at least suggestive that the greatest English Arminian was reared in a village and neighborhood to which active and self-confessed Arminianism had long been no stranger."[2] Of course, this is circumstantial logic at best, but such is the case with the direct connection between Arminius and Wesley. Dredged swamps, journal titles, and correlative examinations are about all we have to go on Some have called the Arminian influence upon John Wesley an "anonymous impact."[3] Whether this is true or not need not discount the thesis that Wesley was thoroughly Arminian, and that Wesleyan theology is, therefore, the practical development of Arminian theology.

Wesley's central teaching was that the followers of Christ needed to know, love, and serve God with all of their hearts, minds, and souls and to love their neighbors as themselves. This message can be described as the message of Christian holiness and, ultimately, Christian perfection, the latter being possible in this life solely by the grace of God. Wesley was concerned that Christianity had become a dead or stale set of propositions and that, accordingly, faith was merely mental assent to such propositions. The goal of Wesley's Methodist bands was to effect deep and personal change of one's heart and soul that would call one out of religious slumber into the passionate and complete love of God and others. As such Wesley was a prophet and a missionary first to England, and then to all of the world. Likewise, Wesleyan theology, by necessity, possesses a distinctly missionary (or missional) and evangelical zeal.

2. Nuttall, "The Influence of Arminianism in England." This address can also be found in McCullough, ed., *Man's Faith and Freedom: The Theological Influence of Jacobus Arminius*, 46–63.

3. McCall and Stanglin, *Jacob Arminius: Theologian of Grace*, 5.

> Among the Puritans of seventeenth-century England not only was any missionary enterprise almost entirely absent but also there was little or no missionary concern. This is apt to surprise us, but our surprise is a measure of the triumph of Arminianism . . . Speaking historically, the missionary overspill of Christianity during the last 170 years would hardly have been made possible psychologically but for the Arminianism of the Wesleyan Methodist movement.[4]

This missional and evangelical zeal could not exist apart from Wesley's thoroughly Arminian theology, focused as it was on the free and universal grace of God made possible by Christ Jesus the Son, through the Holy Spirit. According to Nuttall, "The theology of Calvinism arises, naturally and properly, as a theology of the people of God within the household of God. An Arminian theology arises equally naturally and properly as a theology of mission to the unbeliever."[5] Indeed, fundamental to Wesley's religious reforms, and to subsequent Wesleyan theology, is that all humans are sinners and thus stand in need of redemption. Such redemption has been wrought, once and for all, by the work of Christ and is freely available to all persons. Furthermore, faith in and obedience to Jesus results in the transformation of persons from sinners to those in whom dwells the whole mind of Christ.

Wesleyan theology, therefore, is aimed not only at faith but at living, active, and transformative faith. Such faith draws deeply from the well of Arminius's theological work contra the intensified Calvinism of the supralapsarians. Stephen Gunter has concluded that Wesley's soteriology is "a

4. Quoted in ibid.
5. Ibid.

faithful representation of original Arminianism."[6] I would put it even more strongly, and state that Wesley's theology was thoroughly Arminian as a whole, and that Wesleyanism is the practical flourishing of Arminian theology. Moreover, Wesley's theology, in many ways, is a development of the theology of Arminius. It is, therefore, imperative that Wesleyans return to, or discover for the first time, the works of Jacob Arminius. For it is in Arminius's work that the theological grounding for Wesley's religious reforms can be found. Arminius's theology is more than simply compatible with Wesley's. In fact, it is the bedrock for Wesley's practical work toward religious renewal as well as one of the primary sources for Wesleyanism's missionary and evangelical zeal.

Wesley believed that while none are free from sin, it is equally and more forcefully asserted that none are removed from God's grace, lest they choose to remove themselves, which is itself a divine act of grace toward rebellious creatures.

> If then sinful men find favour with God, it is "grace upon grace!" If God vouchsafe still to pour fresh blessings upon us, yea, the greatest of all blessings, salvation; what can we say to these things, but, "Thanks be unto God for his unspeakable gift!" And thus it is. Herein "God commendeth his love toward us, in that, while we were yet sinners, Christ died" to save us "By grace" then "are ye saved through faith." Grace is the source, faith the condition, of salvation.[7]

6. Gunter, "John Wesley, A Faithful Representative of Jacobus Arminius," 77. Here Gunter states that Wesley desired to distinguish his efforts at revival from the work of the so-called "Calvinian Methodists."

7. Wesley, "Salvation By Faith," 3.

So Wesley says in introducing a sermon on Ephesians 2:8, "For by grace you have been saved through faith, and this is not your own doing; it is the gift of God" (NRSV). Grace is the foundation of creation, and it is God's continual mode of relating to creation. Arminius described grace as the very vocation of God.

> We define vocation, a gracious act of God in Christ, by which, through his word and Spirit, He calls forth sinful men, who are liable to condemnation and placed under the dominion of sin, from the condition of the animal life, and from the pollutions and corruptions of this world . . . unto "the fellowship of Jesus Christ," and of his kingdom and its benefits; that, being united unto Him as their Head, they may derive from Him life, [*sensum*] sensation, motion, and a plentitude of every spiritual blessing, to the glory of God and their own salvation.[8]

Salvation comes by faith in Christ Jesus, which is itself only possible by the free and unmerited grace of God.

Sin, therefore, is the result of human volition. Grace, on the other hand, is the work and result of the divine will to redeem all things. The first "step" of grace, then, is taken by God, allowing the human itself to respond. This first step, which necessarily originates in God, is often called prevenient grace. Subsequent steps are made, cooperatively, by free humans in response to, and in cooperation with, God. "The initial contact of prevenient grace is wholly divine, but the subsequent grace entails a cooperative relationship."[9] As was the case with the view of sin espoused by both Arminius and Wesley, such a view of grace is also in keeping

8. Arminius, *Public Disputation* XV.II.I, quoted in Wesley, *A Plain Account of Christian Perfection*, 23.

9. Stanglin and McCall, *Jacob Arminius: Theologian of Grace*, 153.

with the bulk of Christian tradition. Prevenient grace, for example, is rightfully traced back to Augustine's attempts to combat the heretical teachings of Pelagius. The novelty of this view of grace is the universal role it plays for Arminius and later for Wesley. Grace is available for all: none are exempt. Rooted as it is in the work of Christ—specifically his death and resurrection—grace, and therefore salvation, are truly possible for all. The centrality of this claim for both Arminius and Wesley cannot be overstated. As strongly as can be affirmed, therefore, both are theologians of grace. More than anything else, it is the fundamental disposition of God, as understood by both Arminius and Wesley, to redeem and save sinful humanity by the undeserved gift of grace.[10]

Surely, then, as Wesleyans place more and more emphasis on questions of mission and what it means to be "evangelical," a return to one of the primary sources of our theology—the theology of Jacob Arminius—would significantly aid this process.

FOR DISCUSSION

1. How did the Methodist Church originate, in the United States in particular?

2. In what ways is John Wesley Arminian?

3. How does Arminian theology fund Wesley's "evangelical zeal?"

10. Stephen Gunter, *Arminius and His Declaration of Sentiments*, 7–8.

Chapter 10

ARMINIUS AND KARL BARTH

IN CHAPTER 7 OF this work, we examined Arminius's views on grace, predestination, and election. There we saw that Arminius grounded these doctrines not in the logic of the divine decrees, as did his opponents, but rather in the person and work of Jesus. Arminius's grounding of predestination and election in Christology is a piece of a much larger pattern. Arminius is a highly christological theologian; this is consistently on display in his theology, and surely reveals his highly pastoral convictions. In this way, I believe that Arminius has much in common with another Reformed pastor and theologian who is known for being an outstanding voice for christologically focused reform. That pastor and theologian is the great twentieth-century Swiss theologian Karl Barth.

When the Synod of Dort drew to a close in 1619, one of its greatest accomplishments was the production of the *Canons of Dort* in which the Synod attempted to produce a thoroughly Calvinistic response to the *Five Articles* of the Remonstrants, published in 1610. This formal statement of Calvinism produced by Dort has served to provide shape and clarity to Reformed Theology in general, and Calvinism in particular, even to this day. Likewise, with the production of the *Canons of Dort*, Arminian theology became, essentially, anathema, not only in the Netherlands, but in most of the rest of Europe as well.[1] The five points of Calvinism as put forth by Dort have been conveniently summarized by the acronym TULIP. Those points are total depravity, unconditional election, limited atonement, irresistible grace, and the perseverance of the saints.[2] An investigation into whether or not the "Five Points" of Dort, which are commonly referred to as the "Five Points of Calvinism," are truly the most faithful summation of Calvin's theology is not within the scope of this essay. Rather, suffice it to say, though there are many who have disagreed and who would disagree with portions of the "Five Points," it has remained the decisive statement of Reformed Theology for almost 400 years. The "Five Points" have helped shape and form the tradition of Reformed Theology. Accordingly, most Reformed theologians intentionally try to be faithful to their tradition, using the "Five Points" as a compass of sorts on their quest for fidelity. And then there is the Swiss Reformed Theologian, Karl Barth, who navigates with a decidedly different navigational scheme.

More than anything else, Karl Barth sought to be faithful to Scripture, as it bears witness to the fundamental revelation of God in Christ Jesus. I contend that Barth's

1. For example, Bangs notes that Arminianism was strictly outlawed by the early Pilgrim leaders who sailed to North America and helped found what is now The United States of America. Bangs, *Arminius*, 159.

2. The Remonstrants agree with the Calvinists, for the most part, on total depravity, and they mostly agree about the perseverance of the saints, though they were unwilling to state the matter so definitively as did the Dutch Reformed leaders at Dort. The Remonstrants completely disagree with unconditional election, limited atonement, and irresistible grace, arguing instead for conditional election, unlimited atonement, and resistible grace. Pelikan, *The Christian Tradition*, 232–35.

theology embodies the spirit of the Reformation more than any other contemporary theologian. It might even be argued that he surpasses even Calvin in producing the best statement of Reformed Theology: *The Church Dogmatics*.[3] *The Church Dogmatics*, despite being left incomplete, is a massive testimony to the beauty and power of Reformed theology, and therefore to the *semper reformanda* (always reforming) principle of the Reformation. In short, though I do believe that Barth's theology, for the most part, stands in firm solidarity with Calvin's, and that the Genevan reformer would be proud to see Barth's theology alongside his own, Barth's ultimate goal was not to be faithful to Calvin or to Reformed Theology and its "Five Points." Rather, his goal was to be faithful to Scripture. For that reason, his theology develops and even changes with time depending upon what portion of Scripture he is engaging. Nothing is off limits for Barth, as he will challenge even his own dearest assumptions, to see if they stand up to the litmus test of Scripture. This is something that Barth shares with Calvin, and with Jacob Arminius, as well.

Conversely, this ever-changing and questioning spirit of Barth's theology makes him a rather bad five-point Calvinist, for that system is simply too rigid and inflexible— too unwilling to be challenged and changed by the witness of Scripture. Nowhere can this be more clearly seen than in Barth's radical redefinition of double predestination and, therefore, election.

For Barth, predestination is perhaps the most prominent aspect of his doctrine of God, which can be found

3. A dear friend once related to me a story that was told to him by Hans Küng, according to which Pope Paul VI asked the young Küng about his studies with Karl Barth. The Pope told Küng that, in his opinion, Barth was the greatest example of true Reformed theology since Calvin, perhaps more so than even the great Genevan reformer himself.

in volume II of his *Church Dogmatics*. This is because, for Barth, predestination at its core reveals God's will and purpose in creating, sustaining, and even in redeeming the world in general, and humanity in particular. The focal aspect of predestination, then, is election, as predestination is all about God's eternal choice to create, to be in relationship, and to redeem. Thus the doctrine of predestination gets at the very heart of who God is in God's own self, as it reveals the inner love and logic of God. For Barth, therefore, at stake in the discussion of predestination is none other than the question of the being and nature of God—God's own identity—which, for Barth, is decisively revealed, once and for all, in the person of Jesus of Nazareth. In placing predestination and election under the category of the doctrine of God, Barth states that, "as far as I know, no previous dogmatician has adopted such a course."[4] Barth's penchant for novelty is refreshing.

Predestination, then, according to Barth, reveals the very heart of God. As for Arminius, the heart of God—God's fundamental character—is love. To say that God created some intentionally for wrath, destruction, and utter ruin, and predestined them to be oblivious to God's free grace, as made known in Christ Jesus, is simply unthinkable. This is not to say that God will not allow some to perish. Nor is it to say that God does not know, according to divine foreknowledge, which path, salvation or damnation, individuals might choose in response to God's grace. This is to say, though, that God does not choose prior to creation itself, who will be saved and who will be damned. In this sense, God does not predetermine the entire course of human history. For Barth, therefore, like Arminius, God's foreknowledge does not impede human volition, and yet, likewise, salvation is not to be earned, and is not

4. Barth, *Church Dogmatics*, II/2:76.

the obligatory result of human choice. Yet this is too neat a package for Barth. Left in this way, Barth would assuredly not affirm my description for it is thus far bereft of the one dominant factor that, for Barth, allows this to "work" and also to be faithful to Scripture, in all of its complexity. That one factor is Christ Jesus, specifically, as the object of election. Predestination, especially when understood doubly, can only work when Jesus, the Word of God, the eternally begotten Son of the Father, is the sole object. Thus, Jesus, as truly human, and therefore on behalf of all of humanity, is elect by God to salvation. At the same time, Jesus, as truly God, is elect by God to damnation. As such Jesus shoulders the burden for sin, taking it into himself, even to the point of death on the cross, that in being raised, he is raised victorious over sin and death, the merits of which extend to all of humanity. This allows for true reconciliation between God and humanity. This is perhaps the finest gem of the treasure trove of theology that is Barth's *Church Dogmatics*.

Barth states it as such:

> Starting from Jn. 1:1f., we have laid down and developed two statements concerning the election of Jesus Christ. The first is that Jesus Christ is the electing God. This statement answers the question of the Subject of the eternal election of grace. And the second is that Jesus Christ is elected man. This statement answers the question of the object of the eternal election of grace. Strictly speaking, the whole dogma of predestination is contained in these two statements . . . The statements belong together in a unity which is indissoluble, for both of them speak of the one Jesus Christ, and God and man in Jesus Christ are both Elector and Elect, belonging together in a relationship which cannot be broken and the perfection of which can never be exhausted. In

> the beginning God was this One, Jesus Christ.
> And that is predestination. All that this concept
> contains and comprehends is to be found origi-
> nally in Him and must be understood in relation
> to Him.[5]

This is surely a similar move to Arminius' grounding of
predestination in the person of Jesus, rather than in general attributes of God, such as justice and mercy. To start
with such generalities, indeed to start anywhere but with
the concrete, specific revelation of God in Christ Jesus, is
to commit gross error and to maim one's doctrine of God
before ever getting started. Barth was of the opinion that
much of contemporary theology was so maimed. He was
concerned that it presented a shadowy, confusing, and
misleading doctrine of predestination, and thus that it dis-
torted the very doctrine of God.

Several years before the publication of volume II/2
of his *Church Dogmatics*, Barth addressed this issue with
clarity and precision in one of his Gifford Lectures given in
1938. There, in lecture VII, in discussing articles VII and
VIII of the *Scots Confession* of 1560, he says that the original
authors

> have made it known unambiguously that they
> wish the whole body of material which is called
> the *doctrine* of *Predestination* to be explained
> through *Christology* and conversely *Christol-
> ogy* to be explained through the *doctrine of
> Predestination* . . . They have presented us with
> a riddle and a task which we shall have to work
> out unaided. But we must admit, as in the case
> of Articles 2 and 3, that they have accomplished
> something significant in making manifest this
> relation so expressly, and that they have thereby

5. Barth, *Church Dogmatics*, II/2:145.

presented us with a task which is both significant and fruitful.[6]

Clearly the work done on his Gifford Lectures was
seminal work helping him to lay the foundation for his
monumental Volume II/2 of the *Church Dogmatics*. It was
nothing new, therefore, for Barth to ground predestination in Christology. Barth saw the foundations of such a
grounding in the Scottish Confession of 1560. Likewise,
we have already seen Arminius make a similar move in
1608. The novelty, for Barth, lies rather in the placement of
predestination and election at the heart of his doctrine of
God, and his forceful reimagining of double predestination
in a way that ties up the loose ends that previously existed.
Barth's reimagining of double predestination possesses
none of the qualities of the "fearful symmetry" that Pelikan
observed in Calvin's understanding of double predestination, especially as the doctrine was set forth by the Synod
of Dort.[7] Thus Barth is able to affirm the classical categories
of being attributed to God, predestination—even double
predestination—along with an extremely high Christology,
without relegating God to the willful source of destruction
and damnation for so much of humanity. Barth, like Arminius, was extremely concerned about the image of God
that is portrayed by proponents of limited atonement. He
described the effects of this teaching as casting a confusing and distorting shadow over God and thus the gospel.
Critical even of his own positions, Barth's christologically
grounded double predestination helped move him away
from his earlier dialectical logic—the logic of the "Yes" and

6. Barth, *The Knowledge of God and the Service of God*, 69–70.

7. Pelikan, *The Christian Tradition*, 232.

the "No"—to what I have argued elsewhere is best understood as the logic of paradox.[8] For example, Barth states,

> And we introduce the first and most radical
> point with our thesis that the doctrine of elec-
> tion must be understood quite definitely and
> unequivocally as Gospel; that it is not something
> neutral on the yonder side of Yes and No; that it
> is not No but Yes; that it is not Yes and No, but
> in its substance, in the origin and scope of its
> utterance, it is altogether Yes.[9]

In Christ Jesus, God speaks, unilaterally, from the foundations of the world, an overwhelmingly unmistakable "Yes" to humanity, a "Yes" that elects humanity, despite its prideful sinning, to be in relationship with God the Father, through the Son, by the Spirit. That "Yes" contains within it a "No" but it is not a dialectical "Yes" and a "No," and it is most certainly not a "No," but rather it is a clear and resounding "Yes." And so, "the election of grace is the sum of the Gospel—we must put it as pointedly as that."[10]

Standing as bookends, then, on two very different ends of the Reformation and of modernity are Arminius and Barth, each arguing for quite similar understandings of predestination and election. Each in their own way believes that God has predestined humanity for grace, specifically through the election of God's Son Jesus on our behalf. Both retain the fundamentally Reformed principles of *sola Scriptura* and *sola fidei,* or salvation by grace through faith. Specifically, they both elevate the place of Christology and seek to understand all other doctrines in light of Christ Jesus. Arminius and Barth certainly do have their

8. See Brian, *Covering Up Luther.*

9. Barth, *Church Dogmatics*, II/2:13.

10. Ibid., 13.

differences. Their similarities, though, offer much hope for contemporary theology. It is my opinion that further investigation into the theological similarities between Arminius and Calvin would be welcome and worthwhile.

FOR DISCUSSION

1. What is the TULIP theory? How did it come about?

2. Where does Karl Barth place the doctrines of predestination and election in his theology, specifically his *Church Dogmatics*? Why is this important?

3. Is this comparison of Arminius and Barth helpful and faithful to the theology of each?

4. If so, how might this comparison affect the ongoing impact and interpretation of each?

Chapter 11

CONCLUSION

What Does It Mean to Be
an "Arminian" Today?

THERE IS A GULF between Arminius and Arminianism.
This gulf is somewhat inevitable. It began with the noble
intentions of the Remonstrants who sought to clarify the
great Dutch theologian's thought into a few basic points.
The critical work of those intensely Reformed followers of Calvin who were responsible for the Synod of Dort
widened the gulf. With time the "-ism" bearing his name
became a veritable insult. The gulf between Arminius and
Arminianism has been further stretched, sometimes even
beyond recognition, over the past few centuries.

It is also true that the Oudewater of Arminius's day
could not be more different from the modern/postmodern
world of today. Regardless of the reason, Arminius is not the
first to suffer such a fate, and he will surely not be the last.
Hopefully this book has helped readers to briefly familiar-
ize themselves with Jacob Arminius—the man behind the
adjective. Having examined his life and his major theological contributions, I have attempted in the final section of
this book to examine Arminius's theology in dialogue with
a few other key theologians. I concluded that Arminius

was not a Pelagian, that John Wesley was indeed a faithful Arminian, and that Karl Barth bears many theological similarities to Arminius, and that these are worth further study. If these conclusions are even remotely accurate, then we must conclude that his theology is not only relevant but also helpful in navigating the modern/postmodern world. Arminius still has much to offer those who would seek to read and understand his work. This latter group bears the name "Arminian." Moving forward, I believe we must be quite clear about what exactly it means to be an Arminian if we are to avoid and even out-narrate the unhelpful caricatures that persist. In what follows I will seek to do just that.

As I understand it, there are five key characteristics to Arminius's theology. Any theology that attempts to be "Arminian," therefore, must take these points seriously. First, Arminius's theology was biblical theology. Arminius read and interpreted Scripture. He was far more concerned with being biblically accurate than logically sound. This is not to say that Arminius was a fideist, or one whose theology was illogical. Rather I simply mean to say that, unlike many of his opponents, Arminius refused to begin his theology in logical axioms, insisting upon beginning only with the Word of God. Arminius was a biblical theologian. Arminian theologians, therefore, would do well to base their theology in Scripture, allowing it again and again to inform, challenge, and even change their thoughts and agendas. Arminian theology simply must be biblically oriented if it is to be faithful to Arminius.

The second point can be derived from the first: Arminian theology must also be christologically focused, within a deep and intentionally robust Trinitarian framework. That Arminius's theology was christologically centered is nowhere more apparent than his most important work, *The Declaration of Sentiments*. There, Arminius counters the logical system of divine decrees proposed by his opponents with a christologically based understanding of predestination and election. Jesus Christ—priest, prophet, and king— is the central figure and subject of Arminius's theology. Moreover, in similar fashion to the early church, Arminius's christological theology requires a robustly Trinitarian theology. That God is Triune is assumed on every page of Arminius's work. Jesus is not adopted or chosen, but is the second person of the Trinity, the eternally begotten Son of the Father. Jesus is the mediator for humanity, bridging the gap created by sin and death between the Father and us. Jesus is not *autotheos*, nor for that matter is the Holy Spirit, but the three together are One. Arminius does admit to a preferential place within the Godhead, believing the Father to be first among equals. In this way Arminius is consistent with orthodox Trinitarian theology. God is Triune. The Triune God is fully revealed to humanity in Jesus of Nazareth. We continue to encounter Jesus, and even to be made into his body and image through the power of the Holy Spirit. This was paramount for Arminius. Arminius's theology, therefore, was highly christological within a deep and robust Trinitarian framework. As a result, Arminian theology must also seek to be grounded and defined by its Christology and Trinitarian theology.

Third, Arminius's theology was pastoral theology. Arminius's pastoral nature was clearly on display in the biographical section of this work. The impact of Arminius's pastoral nature is equally evident in his theology. His is a kind, compassionate, and evangelical theology. Arminius was concerned about people, about their souls, and about their very lives. He served the poor, needy, and well-off alike, and did so with great passion for many years. Arminius was a pastor. As such he also cared deeply for the church. He served the church, both locally and abroad.

Arminius took his duties seriously, and sought to serve the church in both his parish and academic work. Arminian theology can only be "Arminian," therefore, if it is done in intentional service to the church. Arminius's theology was not abstract or unfairly critical of the church. Rather, he sought to faithfully serve and edify the church. Arminian theology, then, must take its cue from him on this note and seek to do theology from and for the church. Critique can certainly be a part of this stance, but such critique must always be that of loyal critique. Arminian theology should be thoroughly and quite obviously pastoral theology. It should seek to teach, challenge, rebuke, and encourage the church of Jesus Christ.

A fourth and similar point is that Arminius's theology demonstrates what I call an ecumenical spirit. Arminius was a Reformed theologian; this much is true. It is also true, however, that he strongly disagreed with a few major tenets of popular Reformed theology in such a way as to be involved in very heated theological debates and even controversy. Interestingly, Arminius's theology, in the places where he differed from the intensified Calvinism of his day, moved him close to Roman Catholic positions of grace, predestination, and election. While Arminius was clear to reject Roman Catholicism, the similarities in his theology on these points cannot be denied. Arminius was also influenced by humanism, a movement that was just building momentum during Arminius's day. Perhaps it is best to simply conclude that, while Arminius was a Reformed theologian, he did not demonstrate a strong desire to toe the party lines of Reformed theology. He certainly did not seek to be Roman Catholic either. Instead, Arminius sought to be faithful to Scripture, eschewing the drive to promote a particular tradition over another. For contemporary Arminians, then, ecumenical dialogue, work, and genuine concern is recommended. Embracing Arminius's theology should be less an issue of denominational loyalty and more an issue of gospel obedience, the latter able to connect Arminians with sisters and brothers who might affirm slightly different theological interpretations of Scripture. There is absolutely nothing wrong with denominational loyalty, unless such loyalty places one in opposition to the gospel. Arminius is a prominent example of one faced with such a dilemma who sought obedience to Scripture over a particular denomination or tradition. Arminians, therefore, should seek to be good Christians first and good Anglicans, Methodists, Wesleyans, or Nazarenes second.

Finally, aside from Arminius's strong Christology, his theological signature was his position on grace, election, and predestination. Perhaps more than anything else, this signature of Arminian theology must be the signature of Arminianism. Arminius strongly affirmed original sin and total depravity. For Arminius, humanity's rebellion against God in the garden destroyed the *imago Dei* or image of God, rendering us incapable to do good on our own. That being the case, though, God deemed it inexcusable to allow humanity to remain in this cursed state. And thus solely as a result of God's grace manifested in the covenant and ultimately in the death and resurrection of Jesus of Nazareth, God restored to humanity that which we could not recover on our own. (John Wesley affirmed the same.) As a result, humans are to a certain extent free—free to choose, yes. Though perhaps it might be best to think along the Arminian terms of being a vessel. Humans are vessels. By God's grace humans can choose to be open to God or closed to God. In the latter instance, the choice to be closed to God is the choice to reject God, or the choice of damnation over salvation This choice is inconceivable and yet all too prominent for Arminius. The former, though, is not the cause that results in salvation. Salvation is most certainly not the result of human choice for Arminius. Rather, in choosing to be open to God, the Triune God grants faith and ultimately salvation to a person. Salvation begins and ends with God's grace for Arminius. Within this scheme, however, human agents do have a choice: a choice to either be open to God or closed to God. This choice is not ours by right but by gift. For Arminius, God predetermined from the beginning of time to save all people through the election of God's Son Jesus—electing him to take upon himself our sin, and electing humanity to assume the grace and holiness of Christ. The end result of the this election is that God triumphs over sin, and that humanity receives by free gift the limitless grace and love of God, resulting in salvation. As a result of this understanding of predestination and election, humans are freed. Some claim, therefore, that it is helpful to think of human freedom or free will in terms of freed will. This is most assuredly a helpful category to think within.

Salvation is thus possible, though not guaranteed or owed, to all people according to Arminius. For this reason, Arminianism should be categorized by a radical optimism of grace. None are beyond salvation, for the free gift of grace has been and continues to be extended to all. No one is off limits; there are no boundaries God's grace is unwilling to cross. All were predestined for election. We must choose, however. Arminian theology should be fundamentally characterized by a desire to see all people open themselves to God. Likewise Arminian theology should strongly affirm God's utter sovereignty, for God alone is the one who makes salvation possible. Finally, Arminian theology affirms human freedom, albeit in a limited sense. We are free to choose. Yet that freedom rightly needs the guidance of the Holy Spirit, the community of faith, Scripture, and an obedient life of holiness. Arminian theology should seek to foster the role of all of these holy influences upon believers. Arminianism should strive to love God and love others. Nothing else will suffice.

With this final point comes the challenge of how Arminianism is to respond to evil. What does a thoroughly Arminian theodicy look like? I would argue that an intentionally Arminian theodicy is one that seeks neither to explain away evil, nor simply to ignore it. Rather, an intentionally Arminian theodicy seeks to understand evil for what it is: an abomination of God's goodness. God is not the author of evil according to Arminius. Evil is a privation of the good, and not an entity on its own. Evil has a beginning and it has an ending. God is both *a se*, or without beginning, and eternal, or without end. Evil is our doing, not God's. We should not, therefore, seek to explain evil by including it in God's plan. God does not will evil. God does not cause evil. God allows it, temporarily, while God is wooing us toward God's self. On the cross the death toll for evil was rung, its ending begun. In this time between the times, then, evil roams about like a raging lion, chaotically spilling over the brim, causing destruction, mayhem, and death wherever possible. It does so because it knows its days are numbered. We must endure. We must hope. We must love. We must worship the one who is light and in whom there is no darkness. Arminianism affirms that God is not the author of evil. Arminianism, then, is concerned with the author of grace, for grace is far more powerful, effective, and enduring than is evil.

This is not an exhaustive list. I believe, though, that if Arminianism is to endure, throwing off the caricature and living into the true theology of Jacob Arminius, then it must embrace the these five things. Arminianism must be theology that is biblically based, christologically focused within a robust doctrine of the Trinity, pastoral, ecumenical, and it must affirm God's utter sovereignty while also affirming human free or freed will. With this, of course, comes an embrace of Arminius's signature understanding of grace, predestination, and election. Hopefully a much more grace-dependent theodicy will result, as well. Through the embrace of these theological points I believe that there is hope to traverse the gulf between Arminianism and Arminius's own theology. Such a journey is, I believe, both helpful and necessary as Arminius has much left to say to the church today.

FOR DISCUSSION

1. What are the five key characteristics of Arminius's theology according to the author?

2. How is "freed will" a helpful corrective to the oft-misunderstood "free will?" How is the former a more faithful understanding of Arminius's theology?

3. According to the author, how should Arminians respond to evil today?

BIBLIOGRAPHY

Aquinas, Thomas. *Summa Theologica*. Vol. 1. Translated by the Fathers of the English Dominican Province. Notre Dame, IN: Christian Classics, 1948.

Arminius, Jacobus. *The Works of Arminius*. Vol. 1. Translated by James Nichols. London: Longman et al., 1825.

———. *The Works of Arminius*. Vol. 2. Translated by James Nichols. London: Longman et al., 1828.

———. *The Works of Arminius*. Vol. 3. Translated by William Nichols. London: Baker, 1875.

Bangs, Carl. *Arminius: A Study in the Dutch Reformation*. Nashville: Abingdon, 1971.

Barth, Karl. *Church Dogmatics*. Vol. II/2, *The Doctrine of God*. Edited by Geoffrey W. Bromiley and Thomas F. Torrance. Translated by Geoffrey W. Bromiley. New York: T. & T. Clark, 2004.

———. *The Knowledge of God and the Service of God according to the Teaching of the Reformation: Recalling the Scottish Confession of 1560*. Translated by J. L. M. Haire and Ian Henderson. London: Hodder and Stoughton, 1938.

Basil, *On the Holy Spirit*. Translated by David Anderson. New York: St. Vladimir's Seminary Press, 1980.

Boer, William den. *God's Twofold Love: The Theology of Jacob Arminius (1559–1609)*. Translated by Albert Gootjes. Germany: Vandenhoeck & Ruprecht, 2010.

Brandt, Caspar. *The Life of James Arminius*. Translated by John Guthrie. London: Ward, 1854.

Brian, Rustin E. *Covering Up Luther: How Barth's Christology Challenged the Deus Absconditus That Haunts Modernity*. Eugene, OR: Cascade, 2013.

Bruyn, Theodore de, trans. *Pelagius's Commentary on St. Paul's Epistle to the Romans*. Oxford: Oxford University Press, 1993.

Calder, Frederick. *Memoirs of Simon Episcopius, Vol I–II*. London: Hayward and Moore, 1838.

Calvin, Jean. *Institutes of the Christian Religion*. Edited by John T. McNeill. Translated by Ford Lewis Battles. Library of Christian Classics 20–21. Louisville: Westminster John Knox, 1960.

Clarke, F. Stuart. *The Ground of Election: Jacobus Arminius' Doctrine of the Work and Person of Christ*. Milton Keynes, UK: Paternoster, 2006.

Ellis, Mark A., ed. and trans. *The Arminian Confession of 1621*. Princeton Theological Monograph. Eugene, OR: Pickwick, 2005.

Els, Herbert Dean. "The Christology of James Arminius." MA thesis, Pasadena College, 1958."

Forlines, F. Leroy. *Classical Arminianism: A Theology of Salvation*. Nashville: Randall House, 2011.

González, Justo. *A History of Christian Thought*. Vol. 3. Nashville: Abingdon, 1975.

Gunter, W. Stephen. *Arminius and His Declaration of Sentiments: An Annotated Translation with Introduction and Theological Commentary*. Waco, TX: Baylor University Press, 2012.

———. "John Wesley, A Representative of Jacobus Arminius." *Wesleyan Theological Journal* 42, no. 2 (2007) 65–82.

Harrison, A. W. *The Beginnings of Arminianism to the Synod of Dort*. London: University of London Press, 1926.

Hicks, John Mark. "The Theology of Grace in the Thought of Jacobus Arminius and Philip Van Limborch: A Study in the Development of Seventeenth-Century Dutch Arminianism." PhD diss., Westminster Theological Seminary, 1985.

McCall, Thomas H., and Keith D. Stanglin. *Jacob Arminius: Theologian of Grace*. New York: Oxford University Press, 2012.

McCullough, Gerald O., ed. *Man's Faith and Freedom: The Theological Influence of Jacobus Arminius*. Nashville: Abingdon, 1962.

McGonigle, Herbert Boyd. *Sufficient Saving Grace: John Wesley's Evangelical Arminianism*. Carlisle, UK: Paternoster, 2001.

Muller, Richard A. *God, Creation, and Providence in the Thought of Jacobus Arminius: Sources and Directions of Scholastic Protestantism in the Era of Early Orthodoxy*. Grand Rapids, MI: Baker, 1991.

Nuttall, Geoffrey F. "The Influence of Arminianism in England." An address presented to the Arminius Symposium, Holland, 1960. http://evangelicalarminians.org/the-influence-of-arminianism-in-england (accessed May 8, 2013).

Olson, Roger E. *Arminian Theology: Myths and Realities*. Downers Grove, IL: InterVarsity 2006.

Pelikan, Jaroslav. *The Christian Tradition: A History of the Development of Doctrine*. Vol. 4, *Reformation of Church and Doctrine*. Chicago: University of Chicago Press, 1985.

Slaatte, Howard A. *The Arminian Arm of Theology: The Theologies of John Fletcher, First Methodist Theologian, and His Precursor James Arminius.* Washington, DC: University Press of America, 1977.

Smith, Sherl Dow. "The Distinctive Teachings of James Arminius as Embodied in His 'Declaration of Sentiments.'" MA thesis, Pasadena College, 1951.

Stanglin, Keith D. *Arminius on the Assurance of Salvation: The Context, Roots, and Shape of the Leiden Debate, 1603–1609.* Boston: Brill, 2007.

———. *The Missing Public Disputations of Jacobus Arminius: Introduction, Texts, and Notes.* Boston, MA: Brill, 2010.

Stanglin, Keith D., Mark G. Bilby, and Mark M. Mann., eds. *Reconsidering Arminius: Beyond the Reformed and Wesleyan Divide.* Nashville, Abingdon, 2014.

Vance, Laurence M. *The Other Side of Calvinism.* Pensacola, FL: Vance, 1991.

Wagner, John D., ed. *Arminius Speaks: Essential Writings on Predestination, Free Will, and the Nature of God.* Eugene, OR: Wipf and Stock, 2011.

Watkin-Jones, Howard. *The Holy Spirit from Arminius to Wesley: A Study of Christian Teaching concerning the Holy Spirit and His Place in the Trinity in the Seventeenth and Eighteenth Centuries.* London: Epworth, 1929.

Weiss, William Sidney. "A Study of the Early Church's (A.D. 100–A.D. 500) Relationship to James Arminius' Doctrine of Predestination: An Investigation into the Teachings of Certain Leading Theologians of the Early Church as Background Material for the Chief Tenets of James Arminius' Theology." MA thesis, Pasadena College, 1959.

Wesley, John. "Letter to John Newton." 14 May 1765. John Wesley Letters at Bridwell Library. http://digitalcollections.smu.edu/cdm/ref/collection/jwl/id/44 (accessed March 11, 2015).

———. *A Plain Account of Christian Perfection.* Vancouver: Eremitical, 2009.

———. "Salvation By Faith." Wesley Center Online. http://wesley.nnu.edu/john-wesley/the-sermons-of-john-wesley-1872-edition/sermon-1-salvation-by-faith/ (accessed May 27, 2013).

www.ingramcontent.com/pod-product-compliance
Lightning Source LLC
Chambersburg PA
CBHW030843090426
42737CB00009B/1090